Jimmy Ro

The Man Who Envied Women

Jimmy Robert

The Man Who Envied Women

Bierke Verlag

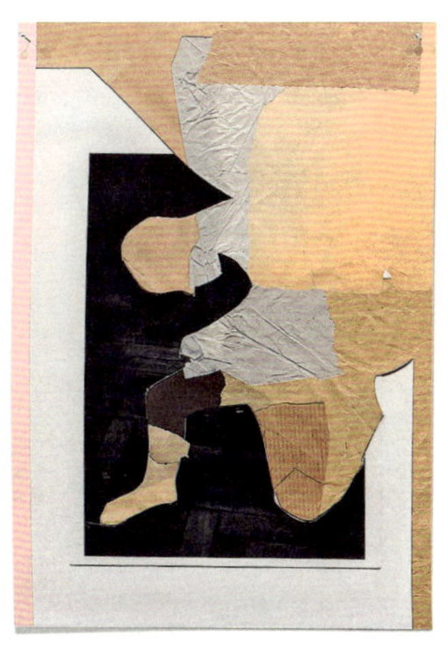

Untitled (Tillmans), 2018

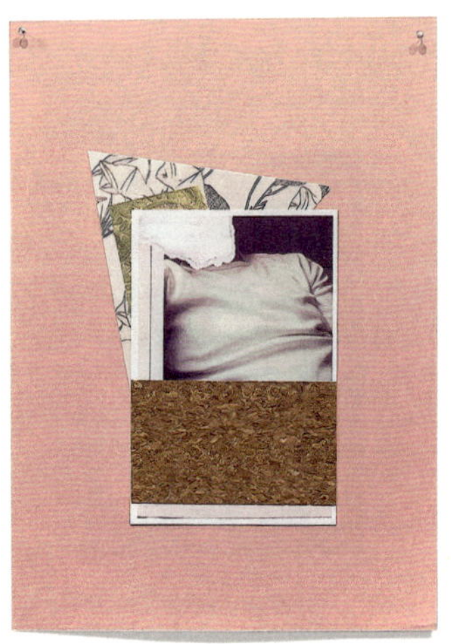

Untitled (Cork), 2018

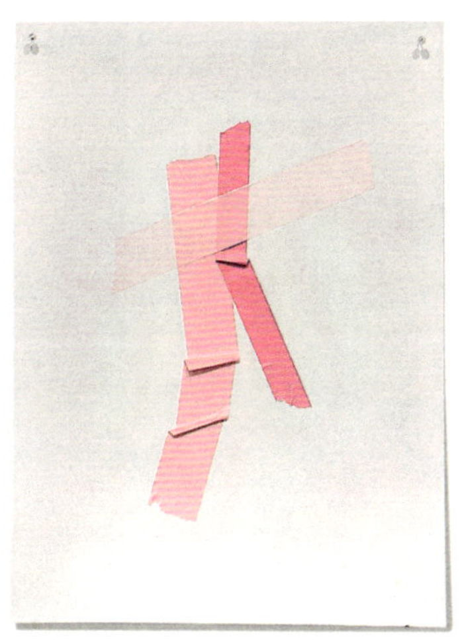

Untitled (Masking tape), 2018

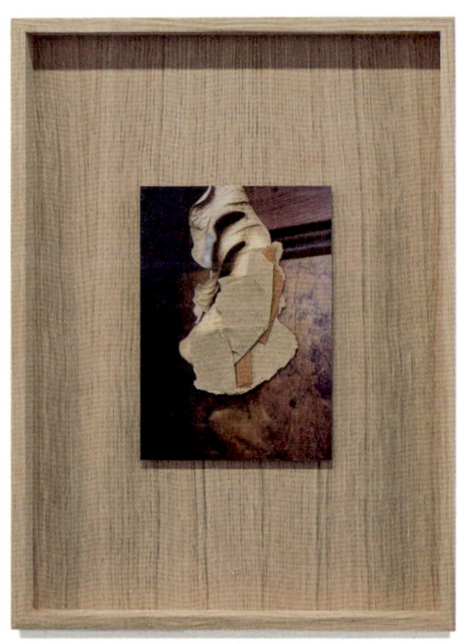

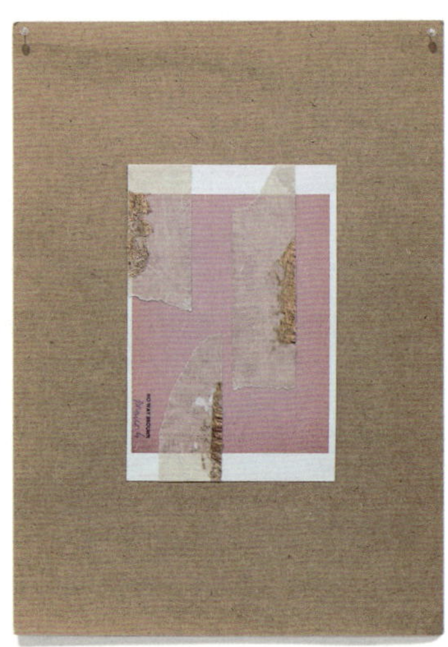

Untitled (Leaf) | *Untitled (Copper)*, 2018

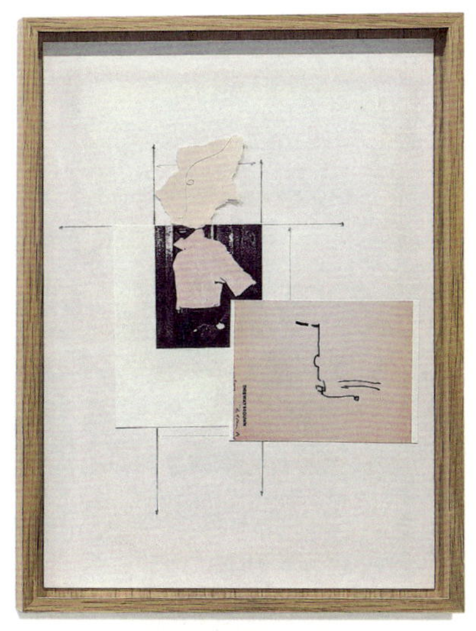

Untitled (Boy), 2018

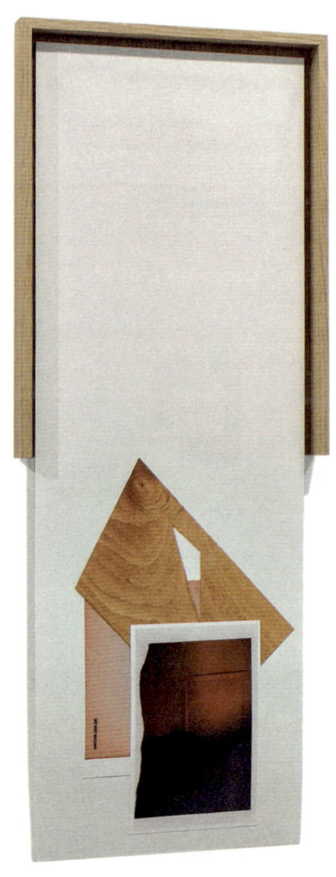

Untitled (Shadows), 2018

Affectional Leaps

Karolin Meunier

An essential moment of dance, of the desire to dance and the desire to watch dancers, is the experience of gravity, which stabilizes the body in space, pulls it to the ground, and yet allows for movements of ascent, even floating. The desired body, the exuberant body, the trained body, the sick body, the supportive body, the overlooked body, and the familiar body and its loss are more than just motifs in Jimmy Robert's *Joie noire* (2019). Robert performs the work with US dancer Courtney Henry,[1] using a joint repertoire that includes movements from classical ballet and pop culture. Over an hour, they take the audience through a series of states that seem either too heavy or too light, depicting or provoking both emotional closeness and historical distance to the themes they negotiate.

Robert's work is often characterized by intense collaborations that bring their own questions and dynamics: the collaborators give each other space but also learn

1 Courtney Henry is a dancer who has worked with numerous choreographers as well as developing her own dance projects, having been classically trained in Florida and New York.

something together, assert something, or enable mutual visibility. Referencing and collaboration are repeatedly felt as form-giving gestures, and these gestures allude to a time before and after the performance, to decisions made primarily in terms of dialogue rather than representation. *Joie noire* is dedicated to Robert's friendship with Ian White, who died in 2013, and is thus a continuation of the moments in which the two artists performed together in public. In its initial performance at KW Institute for Contemporary Art in Berlin, *Joie noire* was part of a series, curated by Mason Leaver-Yap, of contributions by three artists closely associated with White and his work as an artist, film curator, and writer.[2] Leaver-Yap's invitation included a proposal to further consider and share reciprocal influences and engagement. Robert, Emma Hedditch, and Every Ocean Hughes each activated the rooms of KW over two days, and each used different artistic strategies to take a look at the institution itself. In 2012, Robert/White had written of their joint performances: "By this time we were dramatizing *friendship*. Which is always a risk—not least to friendship itself, which is private."[3] The

2 The three events curated by Mason Leaver-Yap under the title *After Ian White* in 2019 were: Jimmy Robert, *Joie noire,* January 19–20; Emma Hedditch, *+49 30 243459-53*, May 18–19; and Every Ocean Hughes, *Help the Dead,* August 24–25. They were part of the *Pause* series at KW Institute for Contemporary Art Berlin.

3 Jimmy Robert/Ian White, "Time/Form(s)/Friendship," in Jimmy Robert, *Vis-à-Vis*, exhibition catalog (Museum for Contemporary Art Chicago, 2012).

constellation of artists at KW likewise reflected friendships, and their "dramatizations" were about understanding and working through the spaces in which intimate, collaborative, or economic relationships emerge, and how such relationships are shaped by those spaces.

I have encountered the work of Em, Jimmy, Ian, and some of the other artists and writers mentioned here in many places in recent years, and have come close to them in different ways, as a viewer and reader, as a friend, in conversation, in writing, and in shared public moments. My description of this performance indirectly gathers impressions that jump around in time.

Before entering the building, the audience is divided into two groups by KW staff and led at different moments through a side entrance into a basement bar. It is dark and Jessica Mitford's critical essay on funeral practices in the US, "Behind the Formaldehyde Curtain" (1963), read by Ian White, plays over loudspeakers.[4] Moved by what we have just heard, we are released into the large exhibition space, bathed in blue disco light and slowly filling with mist. Here we wait. This prelude unfolds the individual elements of the performance through a brilliant sequence that gives them time to appear, overlap, and disappear; the spectators scattered around the space are integrated into this unfolding but have no influence on

4 "Ian, in order to share and discuss [the text] with Jimmy, recorded it on a CD-R." Mason Leaver-Yap, "Boogie Intimacy," in Jimmy Robert, *Call and Response* (Künstlerhaus Bremen/Apparent Extent/Bierke Verlag)

its course. When the two performers appear, descending a staircase, attention and physical presence immediately shift. The spatial center shifts almost magnetically in their direction. Robert and Henry, dressed as doubles, often mirroring and complementing each other in their movements, are turned toward each other in complicity rather than in reproducing the heterosexual figure of a classical dance couple. At several stations, highlighted by light, movement, and the shifting of the viewer's gaze, the fading in and out of sound, dance, reading, and photography invokes and put into relation various references and materials.

These include an intermittently recorded remix by sound artist and DJ Ain Bailey. Bailey has coined the term "acoustic biography" for her work exploring the role of sound in the activation of memory. Her *Untitled: Disco Deconstructed* (2013–19) consists of dance tunes that have played a particular role in her own biography, such as "Love Hangover" by Diana Ross. For a few minutes, this remix forms the soundtrack for the characters danced by Henry and Robert. Just as the fragments of well-known songs activate our physical rather than our cognitive musical knowledge, the moves they quote touch upon our different levels of recognition, personal connection, or distance. Robert adopts Grace Jones' cigarette-holding pose from the *Nightclubbing* album cover. Kneeling then standing, smoking in the spotlight, speaking Jones' lyrics—*Tu cherches quoi, rencontrer la mort ? /*

Tu te prends pour qui. / Toi aussi tu detestes la vie[5]—it is like a melancholy close-up of the androgynous pop icon. Jones' impressive use of sets, costumes, and choreography to consciously shape her public persona and her visibility as a Black musician in the 1980s appears in the performance in another way: it is in the documentary photographs that the pictorial staging of its individual scenes becomes clear. When asked whether the title *Joie noire* may allude to taking pleasure in disappearing in the dark, Robert replied:

> I am not sure there is necessarily a pleasure in being invisible but perhaps more a pleasure in learning how to make the most out of one's own invisibility, meaning if there is a lack of representation or one does not feel represented, there is still agency in the act of finding ways to challenge this.[6]

Some references only become apparent via the bibliography in the handout of the piece. This includes two lengthy quotes from Douglas Crimp's book *Before Pictures*, describing the emergence of disco culture in New York:

5 Grace Jones, "I've Seen That Face Before (Libertango)," 1981.
6 Jimmy Robert, *Joie noire*, written interview with Jimmy Robert by Eva Decaesstecker for Kaaitheater, Brussels, 2019.

> With disco at its best, dancing is both individual and collective. You might connect with the stranger dancing next to you at a given moment, but it's not a couples thing; it's boogie intimacy, which can be very intense and sexy, but it's usually limited to dancing together for a while before you each dissolve back into the crowd or return to your "partner." In this respect, the innovations of disco mirrored the ethos of gay liberation regarding the expansion of affectional possibility. Coupling was newly seen not as a "happily-ever-after" compact but as an in-the-moment union for sharing pleasure.[7]

The excessive dancing invoked by Crimp in his memoirs, the bodies exerting themselves and sweating, the temporary encounters on the dance floor, can only be felt here indirectly through the choreography and the immersive spatial design. Dissolving the space of stage and audience but not the roles of performer and spectator creates a physical closeness and at the same time a separateness; one's own desire to dance, as well as one's own memories of dancing, meet Robert's specific political contextualization. Performing this echo of past and present club culture in an art institution, he questions the limits of the current affective possibilities of both types of space.

7 Douglas Crimp, "Disss-Co (A Fragment)," in Douglas Crimp, *Before Pictures* (University of Chicago Press, 2016).

In other performances Robert has challenged the hyper-transparent ambience of exhibition spaces almost physically—their brightness, straightness, and glazed walls—to confront himself and his audience with the colonialist heritage and gender stereotypes inscribed within them. This also applies to his performances on stage, not least in the collaboration with White. As Kerstin Stakemeier has written, "White animates his sources in his performances by also conversely applying them to himself. By becoming allegorical himself this way, White lets his references have a life."[8] Some of Robert and White's shared sources are likewise animated in *Joie noire*. On the wall hangs a photograph of a book held open by Robert's hands—it is Gregg Bordowitz's *General Idea: Imagevirus* and we see an image of General Idea's *Black AIDS Painting*.[9] Here the focus is on repressed experiences that deeply affected and changed not only the New York art and club scenes in the 1980s: the delayed, fear-ridden, and state-prevented discussion about AIDS and the brutal marginalization that resulted. In the middle of *Joie noire*, Courtney Henry reads a text, written and complied by Robert, that contains extracts from *Women, AIDS & Activism*, an anthology by the ACT UP/NY Women and AIDS Book Group. The extracts include discussion of Haitian women's experience with

8 Kerstin Stakemeier, *Entgrenzter Formalismus. Verfahren einer antimodernen Ästhetik* (b_books, 2017), 185.

9 Gregg Bordowitz, *General Idea: Imagevirus* (Afterall Books, 2010).

illness and access to sexuality and health. Such narratives were often absent from public reporting and meant to remain hidden in private; the publication of *Women, AIDS & Activism* in 1990 was at once a gesture of listening and an activist act of awareness raising. Henry reads the text from a large screen facing a corner of the space; the screen illuminates her upper body and obscures it from the audience. Occasionally, she strokes the edges of the device and the wall behind her with soft movements, establishing a connection between herself, those present in the space, and the stories of the lesbian women who nursed the sick bodies of their male friends.

> The hands that touch / The hands that care / During the height of the AIDS crisis women and lesbian in particular were among the rare individuals who dared to touch gay men who were dying, most of them very isolated / The hands that touch / The hands that care / Do you know them? / Where do you find them? / Could you be? / The hand that touches / The hand that cares / Touch this skin, this surface / Is it not soft, is it not mine and yours... / Read its lines, history, intimacy / The social distance, the acceptable one / The space that is allowed between you and me / This work was unaccounted for / These hands were invisible / But they were there, they mattered / Writing, speaking and perhaps not doing justice / To an

> action to unleash power / Located in my awareness of you in front of me / and my invisibility / The hands that touch / that care / for You.[10]

Henry gives Robert's text her voice and performs the quotations. No simple answer is given to the question of who represents whom and who is in solidarity with whom. The women's accounts remain singular and relate to different experiences of invisibility, illness, and connectedness.

In many of his writings, White emphasizes presentation as actualization, especially presentation of the moving image. Through his practice of combining films and videos across genres and time, and understanding conversations with filmmakers and viewers as part of screenings, he gave form to cinema as live art.[11] His performances also repeatedly name, strain, or leave the framework of a performance's temporary social proximity: at the end of *Democracy* (2010) he stepped onto the street alone and left the audience sitting in the exhibition space, but *6 things we couldn't do, but can do now* (2004), conceived with Robert, was, among other things, an experimental

10 "The Hands That Touch" is a montage written by Robert and supplemented with a poetic beginning and end with quotes from: ACT UP/NY Women and AIDS Book Group (ed.), *Women, AIDS & Activism* (South End Press, 1990).

11 See Ian White, "Recording and Performing: Cinema as a Live Art/Becoming Object," in Mike Sperlinger (ed.), *Here is Information. Mobilise: Selected Writings by Ian White* (LUX, 2016).

arrangement for spending time together on stage. Their 2012 text suggests that we might be less vulnerable when in company and learn more about our limits.[12] *Joie noire* can also be understood as an experimental arrangement. It deals with loss and absence, yet it asserts presence and continuity because the two artists' exchange was always connected with or addressed other voices.

> I don't believe that the work we were making was solely about us and a private conversation but very much stemming from a desire to open discourse around visibility, representation, desire and what could stimulate autonomy and forms of independent thinking.[13]

This statement by Robert is so tangible in *Joie noire* because the people who make up the audience, as in earlier works, play an essential role: they become part of the discussion by forming a counterpart. The performance is a mode of contact that can be as much of sharing as of resistance. *Joie noire* is a decisively staged balancing act, a poetic reflection on spaces and signs of intimacy and friendship. When Courtney Henry and Jimmy Robert disappear at the end by dancing up the stairs, everyone else is left in and with their own position in space.

12 Robert/White, 2012.
13 Robert/Decaesstecker, 2019.

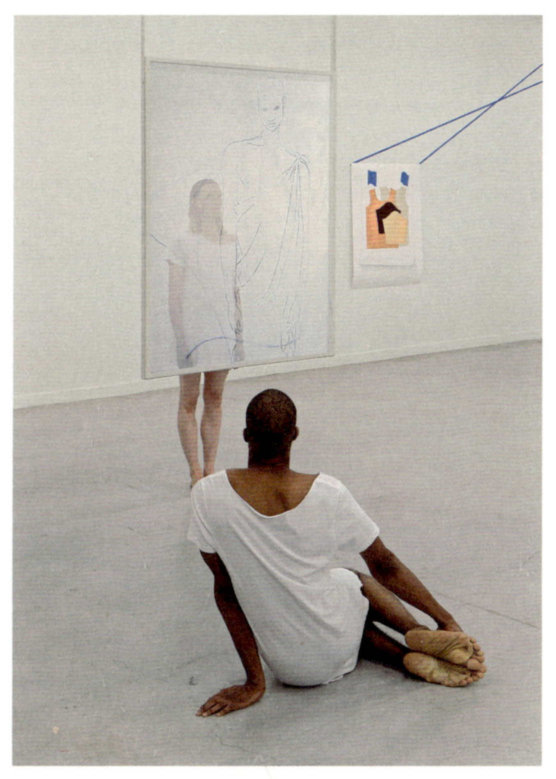

A clean line that starts from
the shoulder, 2015

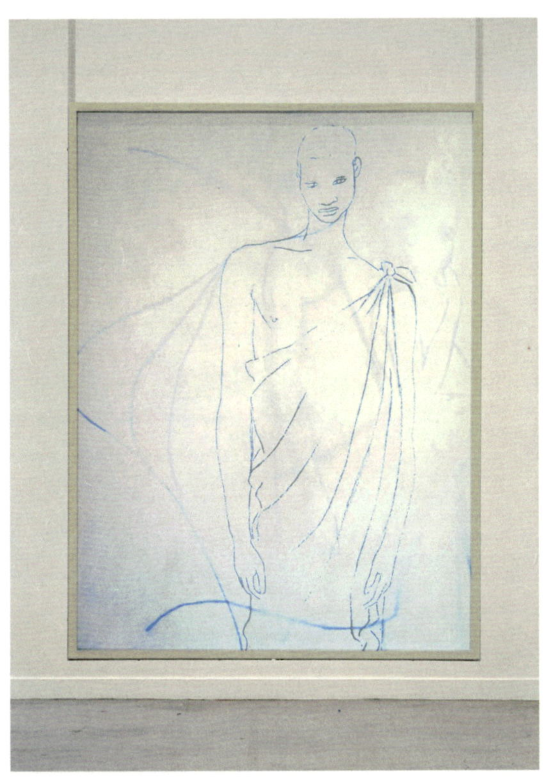

Silk, 2015

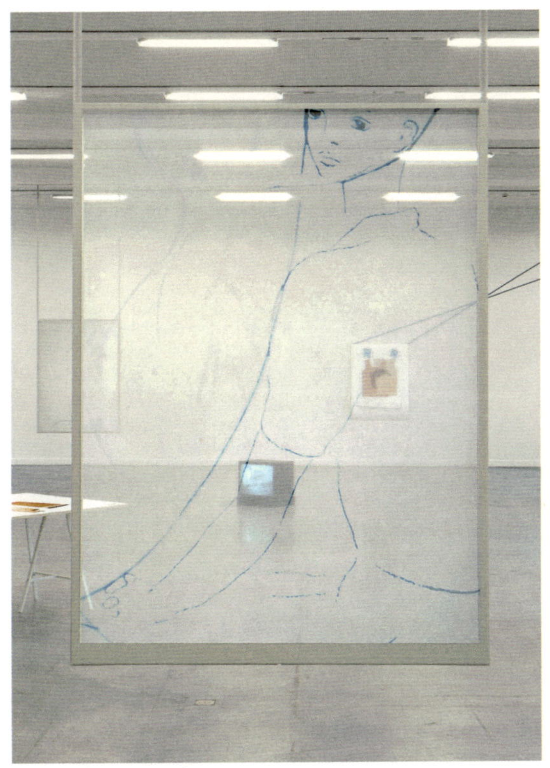

Silk, 2015

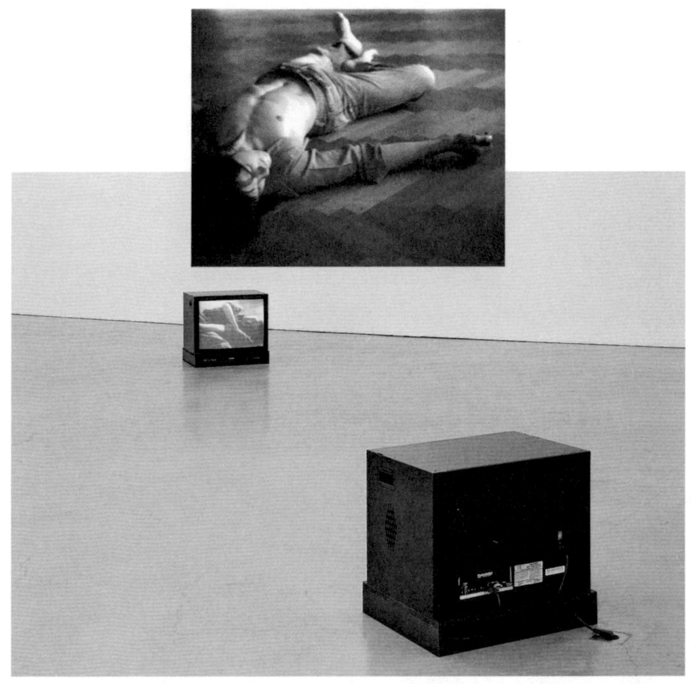

Lili Dujourie
Enjambement, 1976

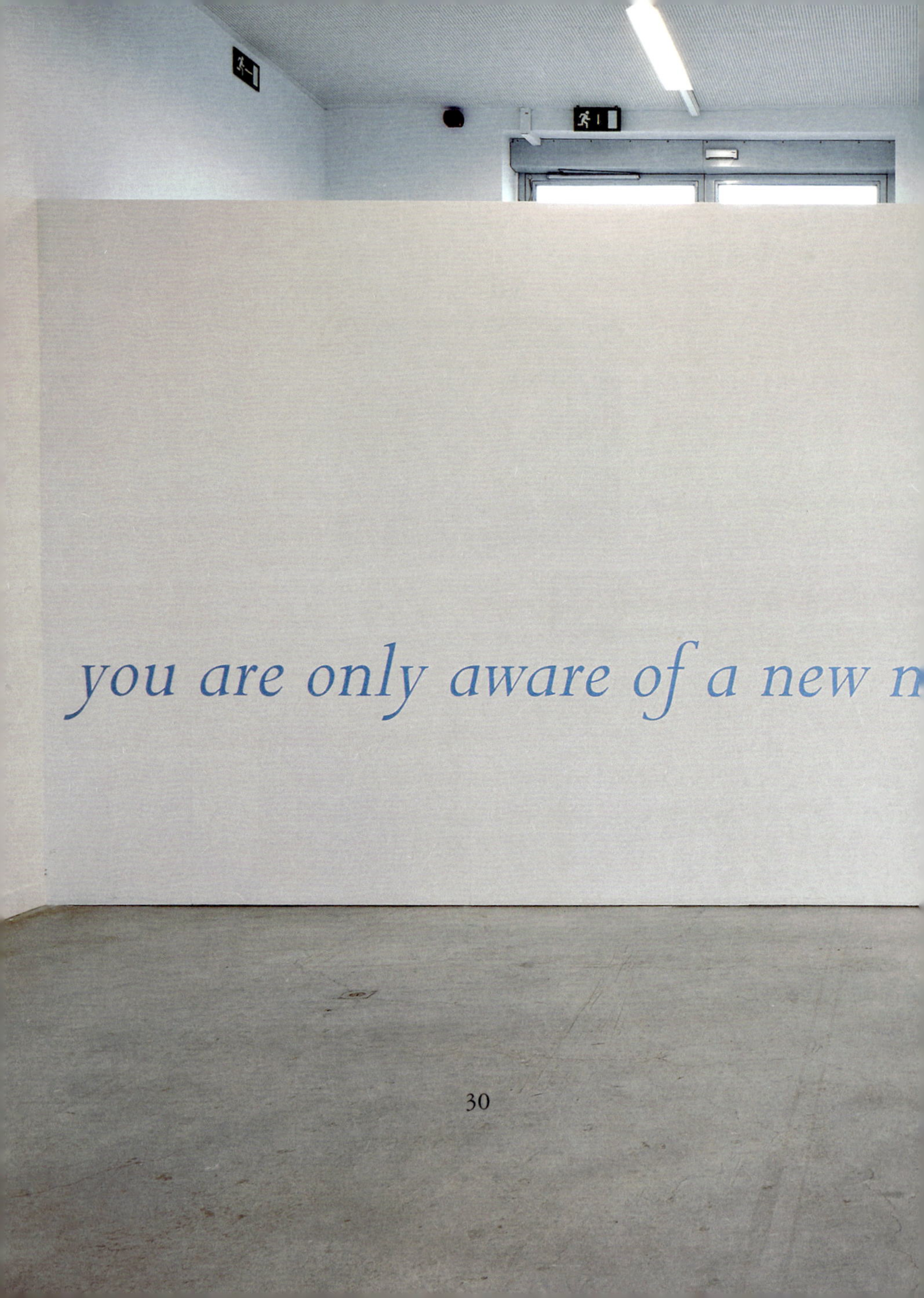

you are only aware of a new n

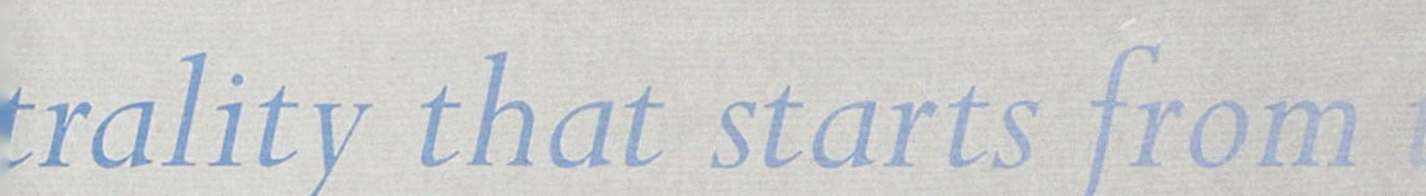

You are only aware of a new neutrality that starts from the hip, 2015

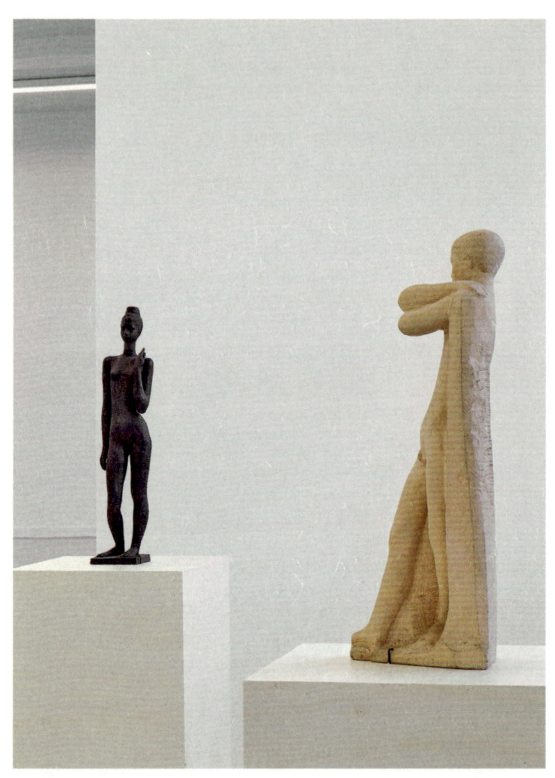

Idel Ianchelevici
Dédée, Jeune fille, 1951 | *Adolescent*, 1951

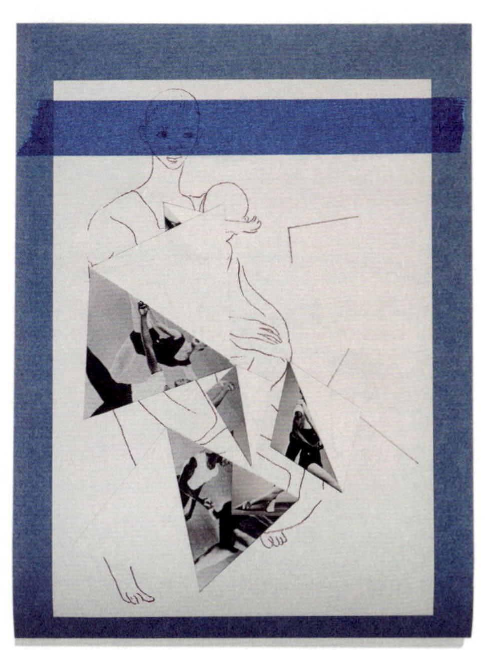

Aegon, 2015

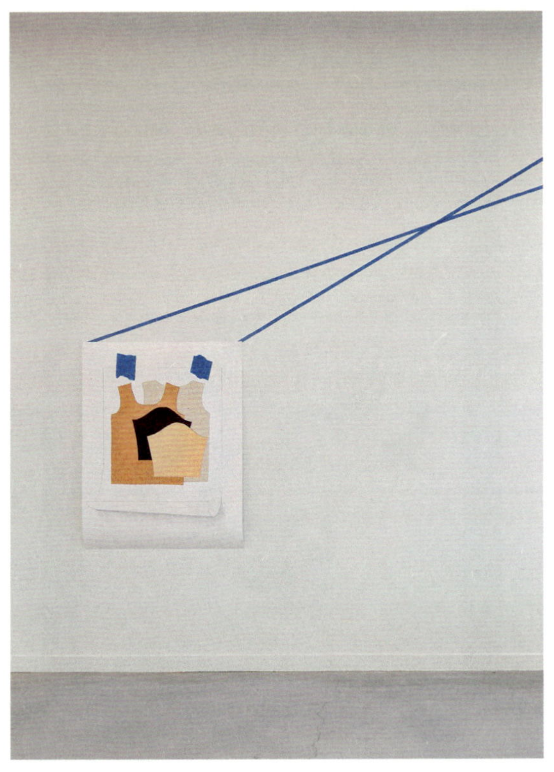

Untitled (Wearing Thin), 2015

Water binds me to your name

As a matter of etymology , the sea came first.
Archipelago, a word borrowed from Italian and before
that, from Greek: arkhi: chief + pelagos; sea.
The chief sea for the Greeks, of course , the Aegean,
a sea that happens to be full of islands.

Archipelago: another name for the Aegean sea, now
used to describe scaterings and clusterings and chains
of islands everywhere…

when Derek Walcott calls the Caribbean the new
Aegean, it is not merely a classical affectation,
but a nearly literal definition of the archipelago

The caress of the water on the skin

The water is dark like me
and it's calling me
Will I resist its call?

heavyness yet lightness

Swimming amongst ghosts
Body to body

Your skin on their skins

Your dead cells enter me
Then you leave me

ينُطبري
لِكمسُاب
ءُاملا
Water binds me to your name

swimming is in itself an achipelagic gesture that
confuses the opposition between land and water:
"Swimming is understood… as natation, an English-
language term that is cognate with the ancient
Greek nesos usually translated as "island" the term
emphasizes equally insular and mainland… not only
looking out to the sea from the viewpoint of land
but also looking out to land from the viewpoint of sea

It is hard to swim in these waters
Knowing what may lie beneath

The porous water
Floating not sharing their weight
Floating: a possibility?

The temptation not to sink
Heavy heart of stone

Mohamed Bezgour, Anpalagan Ganeshu,
Idris Tey, Esawy Rashedal, Lenja Leci
Kalin Mohammed Fati, Khorany Abdulhabib,
Taher Mohamed Zanati, Naji Dohatem
Abdoulaye Ba, Ayse Abdurrahman,
M'manga Soule, Fadwa Taha Ali
More Kebba Dibanneh, Sharmake,
Aboubacar Sow, Veronique Kabamba
Lazragui Khalea, Alfatehe Ahmed Bachire,
Lawend Shamal, Osato Osara
Houseine Traoré, Ayse Abdulrezzak

NN NO Name NN NO Name

ينُطبري
كِمسُاب
ءُاملا

Morocco Sri Lanka Tunisia Kurdistan Albania Iraq
Afghanistan Egypt
Sub-Saharan Africa Senegal Somalia Comoros Syria
Gambia Ethiopia Guinea
Congo Algeria Sudan Iraq Nigeria Ivory Coast Turkey

Maybe we do live in a world of islands which can be seen as: networks, assemblages, filaments, connective tissues, mobilities, and multiplicities...
Maybe the unity is sub-marine?

You may take the boy out of the island, but you will not take the island out of the boy

The horizon as a line to define a space, as measurement, as History
The horizon as a line to represent, or make visible or invisible
The horizon as a mirror

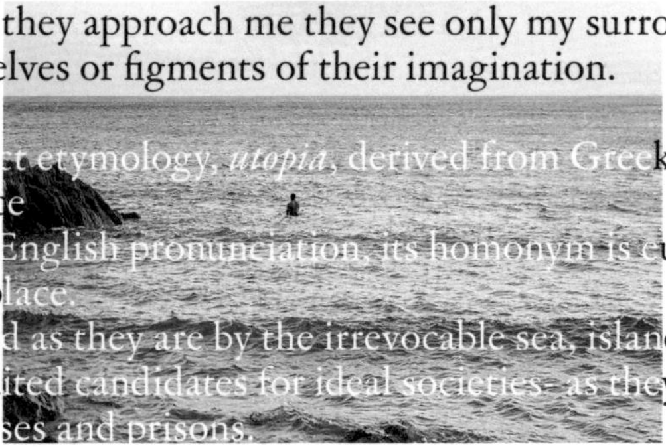

When they approach me they see only my surroundings, themselves or figments of their imagination.

By strict etymology, *utopia*, derived from Greek, means: no place
but in English pronunciation, its homonym is eutopia: good place.
Isolated as they are by the irrevocable sea, islands are well suited candidates for ideal societies- as they are for fortresses and prisons.

Until individuals are recognized as refugees, they must be given asylum, you can't hold them in prison, as this would be a deprivation of human liberty. It is the law, part of the universal Declaration of Human rights.
It is a legal obligation.

Fear create boundaries
Boundaries create hate
Hate only serves the oppressor

Maybe the unity is sub-marine?
Maybe we need a conceptual nation to embrace those without a home.

Floating still The privilege of standing Speaking these words
Choosing these words My limit My incapacity

Yet movements, fluidity, fluidity?
Sketching an escape
yet my feet are anchored
Deep in the water
What lies beneath
Beyond the reflection

The necessity of speaking for others when they are unable to represent themselves, underscoring what gets lost forever, what becomes unknowable when there is nothing left to see.

ينُطبري
باسُمكِ
ءُاملا

One never frees oneself from their mother tongue, the familiar. Anyone who speaks a foreign language speaks it from their own mother tongue, which may be recognizable by an accent, a word or an unusual grammatical construction but also by the gaze and the expression on a face. (yes language has a face) Destabilizing western languages as a force through chosen poetic words is a powerful intention: Language is more interesting when not used in a pure way.

ينُطبري
باسُمكِ
ءُاملا

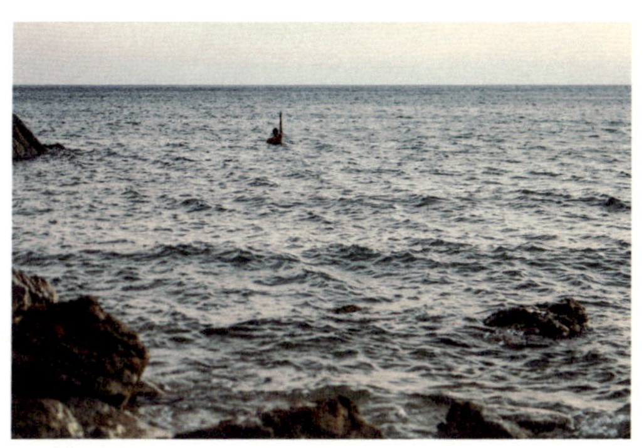

Water binds me to your name, 2022

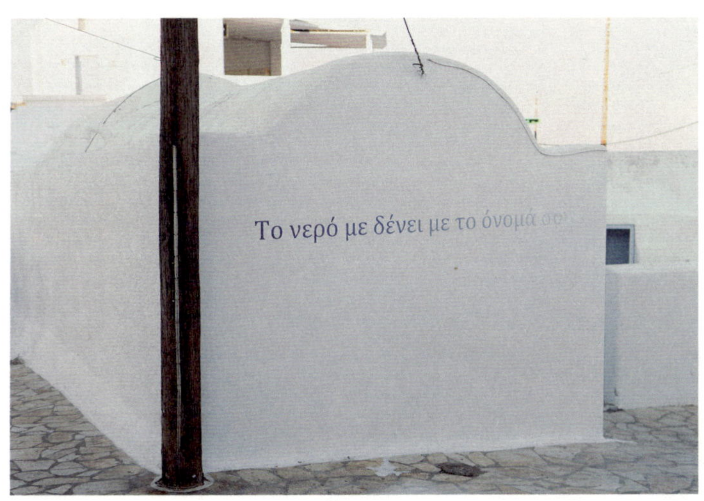

Water binds me to your name, 2022

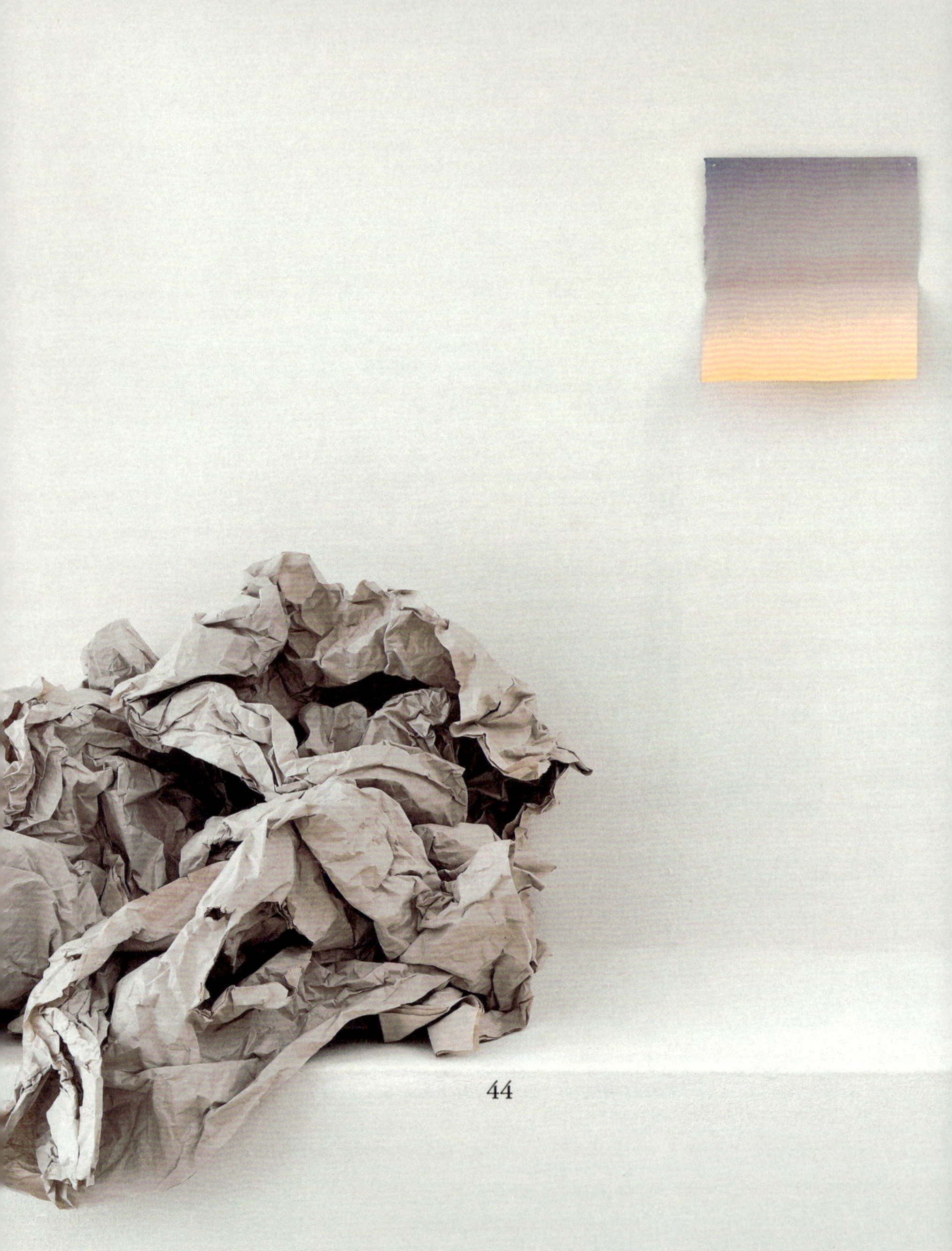

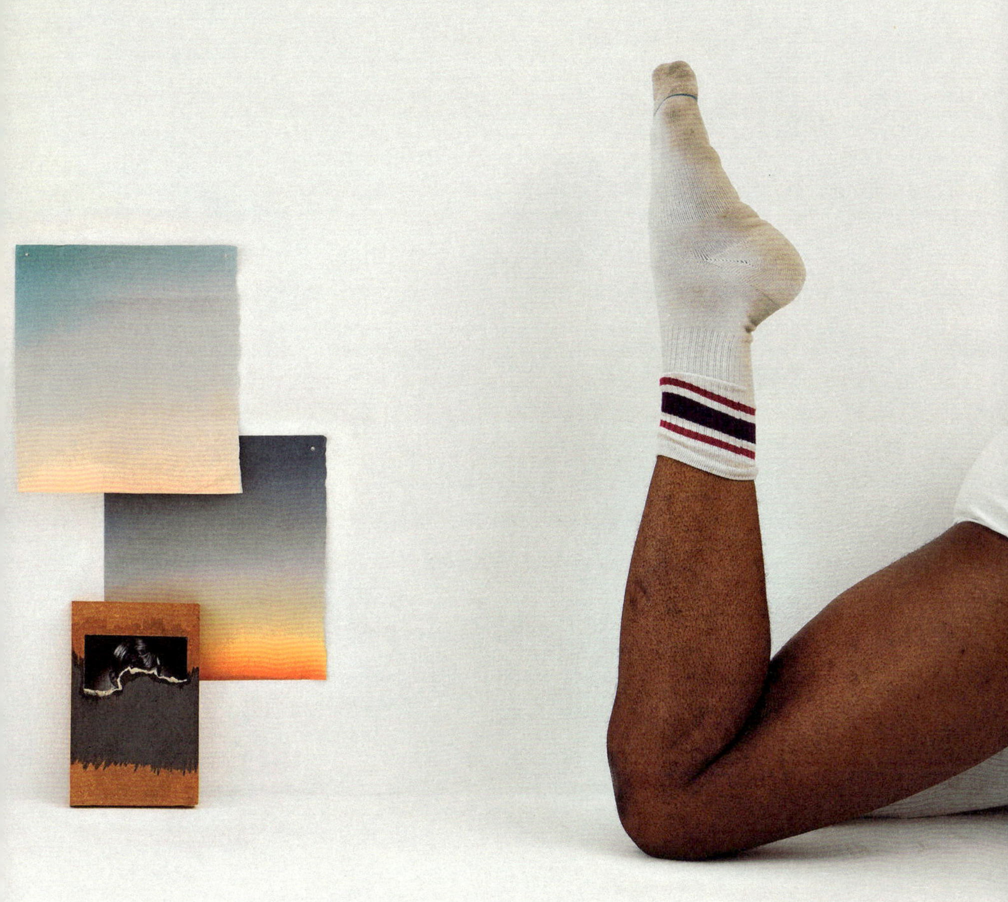

Technique et Sentiment I, 2021

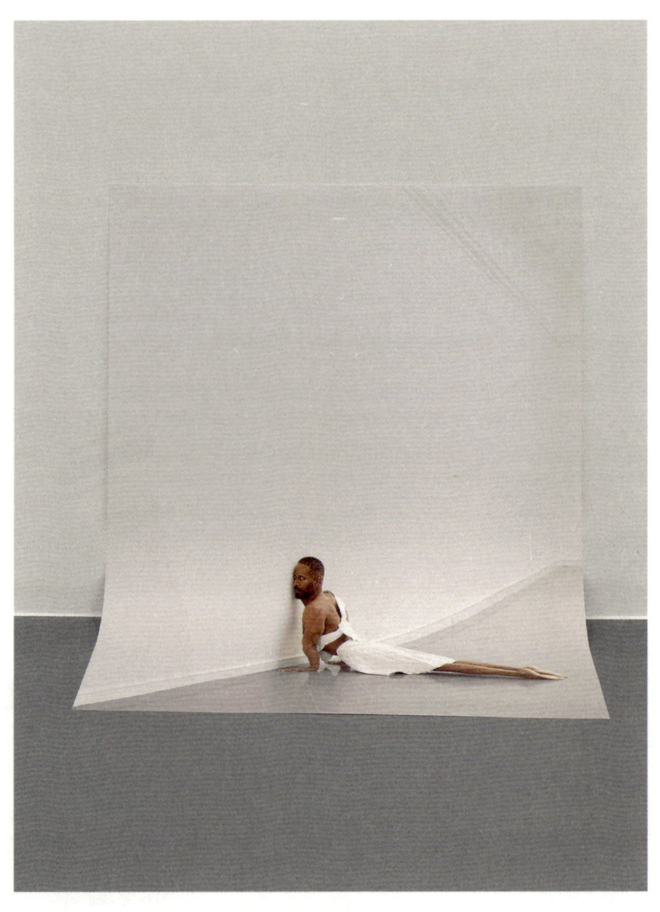

All dressed up and nowhere to go IV, 2024

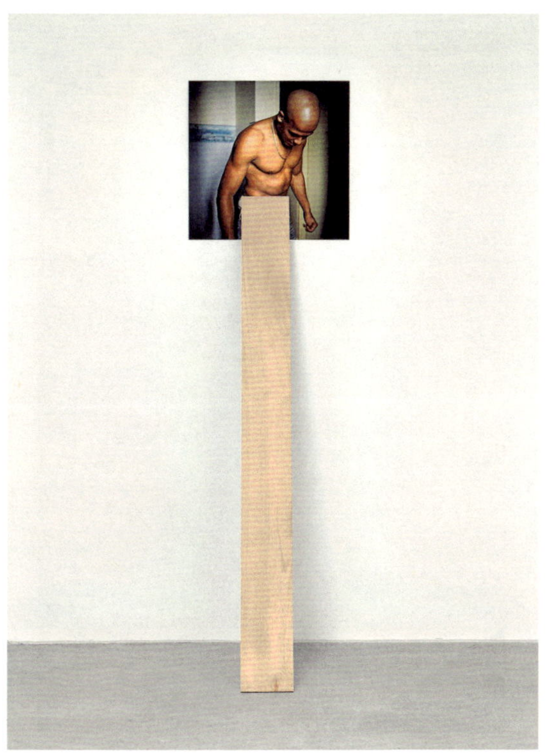

Untitled (Sebastien), 2006

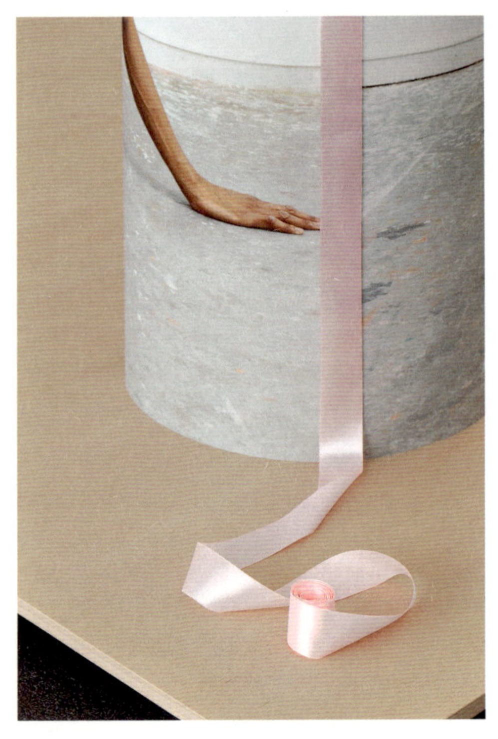

Plié II, 2020

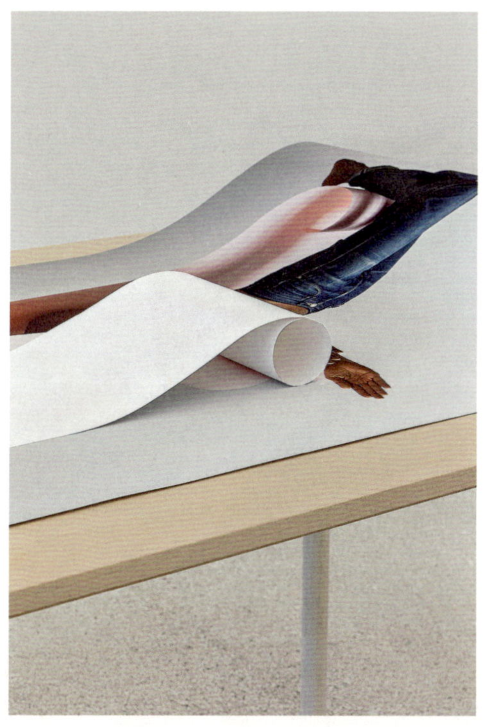

It's not lame... it's Lamé (Toronto), 2016

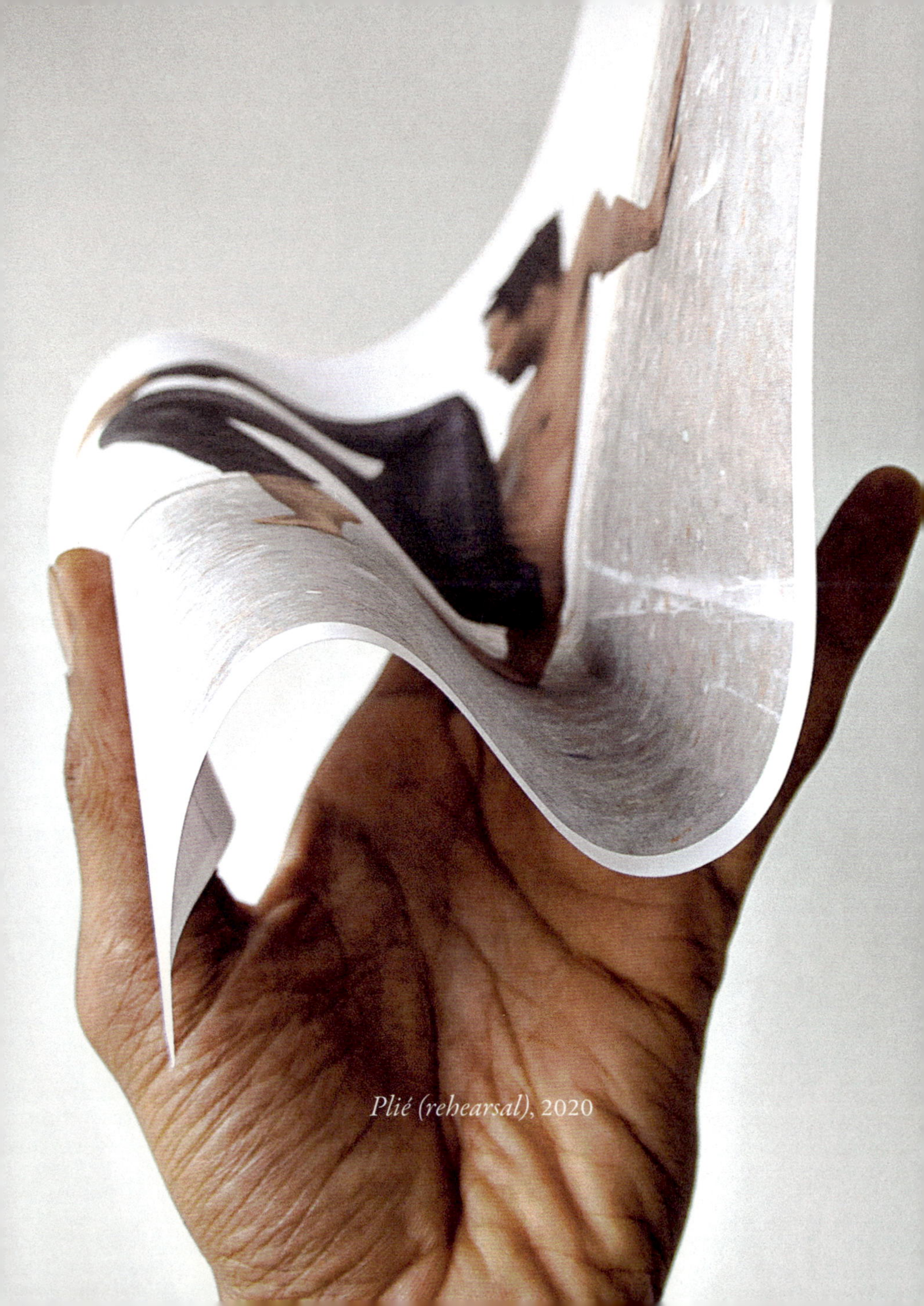

Plié (rehearsal), 2020

A Dis:entanglement

Magnus Elias Rosengarten

to rejoin, to disassemble, to move, to pull, to stretch, to (dis-)orient, to gesture, to alienate, to look, to hold, to embody, to sense, to touch, to restage. This is, in no particular order, an enumeration of verbs, almost the beginning of an artistic vocabulary, that comes to mind when I freely associate with Jimmy Robert's oeuvre. Why begin with words when dealing with an artist who so pointedly employs their own physique as medium and tool in a search for embodiments that materialize differently depending on the power dynamics of each geographic location? Maybe because Robert's work moves at a threshold that is potent with new forms of expression, both corporeal and semantic, that deeply question the unconscious processes of our identity formation in the Western hemisphere. It is a negotiation.

When I received the commission for this text, I wondered how I could engage with Jimmy Robert's body of work, which has been widely discussed in arts publications and exhibition texts. As a writer and curator of German and Ethiopian descent who looks with more distrust and irritation than hope or optimism on the

German art scene (the resilience of German whiteness fascinates me), I found a rather basic question arising in my mind: what Robert's art actually *does* to a European and German art environment. He is in no minor way a significant member of Germany's and Europe's art ecosystems. His gallery, Tanya Leighton, has shown his works in its Berlin location, but Robert also teaches as a full-time professor of sculpture and performance at the Berlin art academy UdK. He participated in the Berghain show *Studio.Berlin*, which ran during lockdown times until August 2021 as a cooperation between the techno club and Boros Foundation. In 2019 he presented the work *Joie noire* at KW – Institute for Contemporary Art Berlin within the performance series *Pause*. It has quite often happened that I learn about Afro-Diasporic artists who practice in Germany not in my home country but while traveling abroad. And indeed, it was upon my relocation to Paris in September 2023 that colleagues of mine introduced me to Robert's work and suggested I meet him, as he and his partner were also about to move back there—to his hometown.

In recent years my research has increasingly sought to comprehend on a deeper level the conditions and politics of visibility, paying close attention to non-white corporealities and embodiments exhibited in European museum and gallery circuits. I am interested in the workings of whiteness to maintain its status quo as it simultaneously attempts to devour artistic positions that challenge such

Eurocentric and hegemonic ideologies. What does a non-white body on a gallery floor, in the context of performance for example, signify in the psychic space of the white European imaginary? Is it possible to elude that almost panoptic gaze?

I read Jimmy Robert's interdisciplinary practice as a gateway that widens sensory perceptions and regards the audience as inevitable participants. It is a tender, empathetic, yet firm position engulfing the optical and metaphysical regimen that whiteness continuously perpetuates. The intrinsic potency of this position plays a significant role in the context of a country like Germany. Considering the small to non-existent presence of non-white German artists or influential curators, which otherwise could form a more complex and nuanced art ecosystem mirroring society's width, Robert hits an afferent nerve of a country haunted by its own history.

In 2019, Robert collaborated with US-American dancer Courtney Henry to present a moving meditation on the legacies of disco and club culture as well as desire and death at KW-Institute for Contemporary Art Berlin: *Joie noire*. Conceived as an homage to the late artist and curator Ian White and organized by Mason Leaver-Yap, their performance involves an interplay of media—from text and sound to photography and movement—and repurposes the gallery space as a blue-tinted disco club environment. Its eclectic mélange of pop-cultural moments and citations, each with its own voice and position, provokes a renegotiation around power and presences, asking whose voices are heard and processed, especially in the context of the AIDS epidemic of the 1980s and ensuing years. Feeling out the affective potentials of the dancefloor, it poses crucial questions: What are the parameters of a body's visibility? Who controls desire? And who, essentially, is remembered? It is never redundant to stress that the politics and discourse of the early AIDS era—despite the innumerable lives it cost—favored and valued queer white bodies over queer BIPOCs. In the middle of *Joie noire*, Courtney Henry introduces a meaningful haptic gesture while reading excerpts from *Women, Aids & Activism,* a text anthology published by the ACT UP/NY Women and AIDS Book Group; the excerpts focus on the voices of women from Haiti living with the virus and the strategies they find to navigate fundamental questions around sexuality and health. Henry reads these passages from the screen of a computer that covers her torso, gently caressing the screen's edges. She also touches the wall behind her, establishing a bodily relationship with the environment and the audience in the room. While touch has consistently played a significant role in Robert's work, I am interested in what those touches might herald or point towards in the space of KW in Berlin.

For US scholar and feminist thinker Hortense J. Spillers, touch "might be considered the gateway to the most intimate experience and exchange of mutuality between subjects, or taken as the fundamental element of the absence of self-ownership… [I]t defines at once, in the latter instance, the most terrifying personal and ontological feature of slavery's regimes across the long ages."[1] Blackness operates across the wide range from the erotic to the most abhorrent perceptual fields; Black bodies consequently often carry such sensory memory which might, in the process of art-making, translate into a particular Black aesthetic. In her tactile engagement with the basement of KW, Henry broke with a normative *white* space that is defining of contemporary art history to open a prism temporarily devoid of one-dimensionality. It was a liberating moment. Her movements sought relationships with the surrounding audience and— for Germany I find this crucial—could imagine, see, touch, and know participants who were German and non-white. What the performance opened up, what Robert invited us into, was a social space that could release performers and witnesses from the hold of *whiteness* for a bit over one hour.

In 2021, Tanya Leighton presented *Technique et Sentiment* in Berlin, an exhibition that primarily focused on Robert's personal archives and elaborated on the relationship between body and space via his material affinity

1 Hortense J. Spillers, "To the Bone: Some Speculations on Touch," *There's a Tear in the World: Touch After Finitude*, Stedelijk Museum of Art and Studium Generale Rietveld Academy, 23 March 2018, keynote address. Available online at: https://www.youtube.com/watch?v=AvL4wUKIfpo.

for fabric, carton, and paper, which often function in his work as stand-ins for the human form. Alongside his photographic (re-)compositions depicting single body parts, partial legs or forearms, was a significant audio piece, *Technique et Sentiment VI*, that was emblematic of the show's integral search for Robert's body. As the listener perceives the artist handling paper, engaging his body by touching, dancing, or stepping on that paper, Robert composes a virtual physicality and seems to gradually reinscribe himself into long-erased or repressed canons. Via the abstract production of a sonically produced body or bodies, he also evaded the burden of singular representations to move towards an omnipresence that shattered the exhibition space. This process of self-creation begins in the imaginative realm and gradually translates into the physical.

Tracing whiteness and its inscription as bodily ideal in art historiographies was also the central theme of Robert's 2022 exhibition *Frammenti* at Thomas Dane Gallery in Naples. Starting with the false belief that ancient Greek sculpture represented the breeding ground and epitome of white European aesthetics, *Frammenti* carefully reconstructed the original polychromatic experience of such statuary. Scientific research of recent decades has debunked the notion of a classical white bodily Greek tradition, while modern technology proves the presence of polychromy—various phenotypes—among the population of Ancient Greece. By positioning classical sculptural works from Naples in immediate dialogue with his own body, mostly through photography, the artist initiated a process of excavating, of historically rehabilitating, a long-hidden visibility.

With its deconstructive characteristic, Robert's body of work carves out and molds intermittently free spaces for experimental relationalities; an inevitable prerequisite for his additional occupation as art professor. In an interview with *Zoo Magazine* in April 2021, Robert said that when it comes to the core of his teaching practice: "I would say that we influence each other [...] I don't want them [my students] to reproduce my work, I want them to be independent artists and thinkers. I want to give them the feeling that they are already artists."[2] Disrupting the idea of the artist working in isolation by stressing the necessary reliance on cross-pollination and co-creation seems to be a central pillar of Robert's teaching practice. Just as he regularly invites artist friends to participate in his work, he regards his students as collaborators as he guides them on the precarious journey toward artistic sovereignty. This is a task, a calling, that is ever more important in times of alarming compromise when it comes to the protection of *Kunstfreiheit* (artistic freedom) and the question of whose positions are deemed worthy of exhibition.

2 Bettina Krause, "Made in Berlin: Jimmy Robert," *Zoo Magazine* 70, Spring issue (April 2021). Available online at: https://www.tanyaleighton.com/content/2-artists/22-jimmy-robert/robert_zoomagazine_april2021.pdf.

An artistic practice and vocabulary that inherently dares to claim its sovereignty and move beyond given social and historical perimeters is of course essential for a culture's vibrancy and survival. Through its semantic and corporeal rehabilitations, Robert's body of work directs us, particularly in the context of Europe's antiquated self-conception, toward a livable future. It moves and unfolds over time; it is in flux and requires our will to surrender to a momentum. It is a frequency and presence that permeates the layers of human existence to liberate many of us from a narrow-minded and flawed European physical ideal. The forms of touch in Jimmy Robert's oeuvre, both metaphorical and physical, resonate with Spiller's deep knowledge and presents as a most intimate offering: intrinsically holding a wisdom ranging from the most brutal and destructive human behavior to the most binding and elevating expression; a touch that allows for visceral adventures that train the onlooker, the participant, in wholesome perceptions—both affectively and visually—that refract from a hegemonic white gaze.

European Portraits, 2017 →

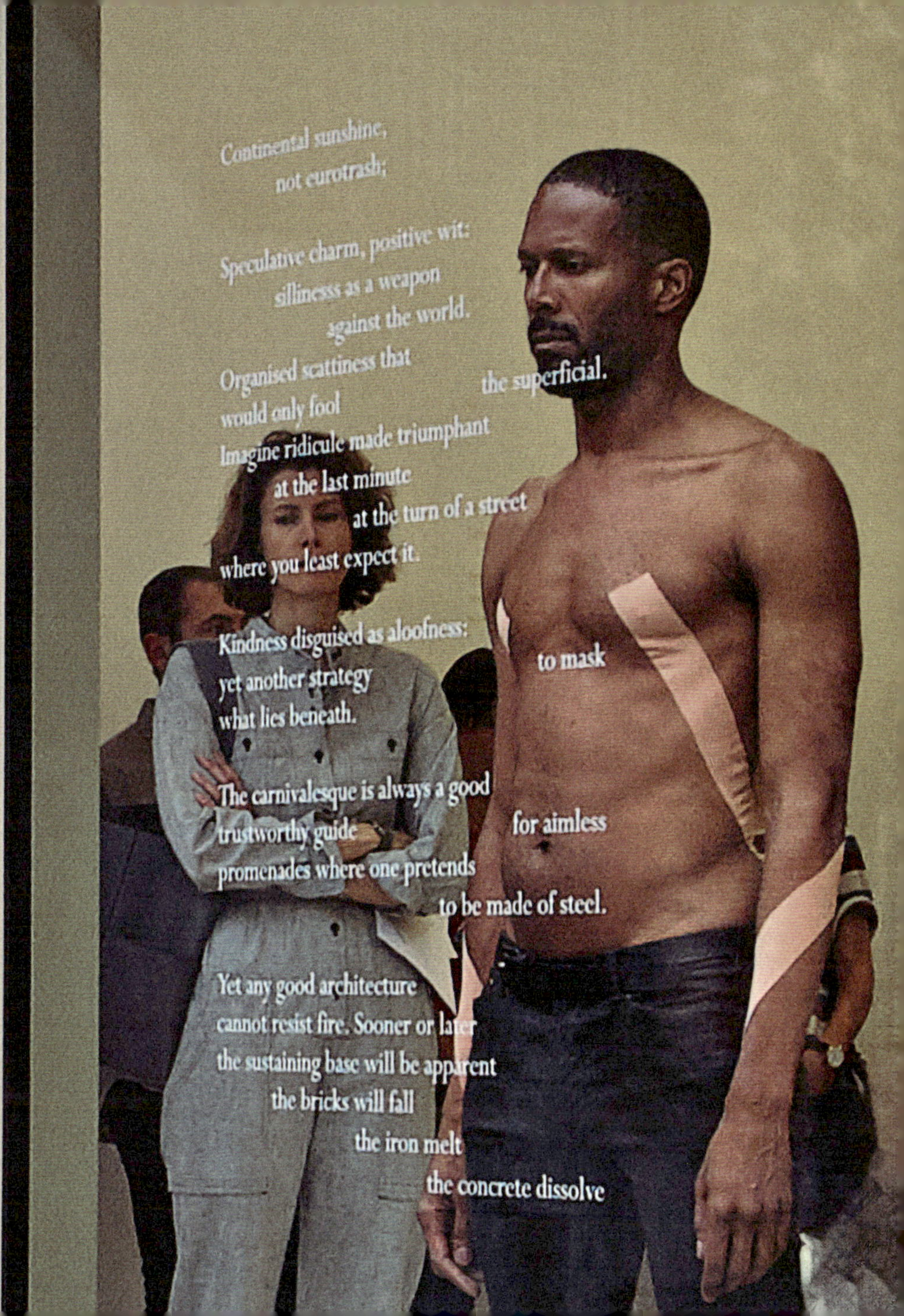

Continental sunshine,
not eurotrash;

Speculative charm, positive wit:
sillinesss as a weapon
against the world.
Organised scattiness that
would only fool the superficial.
Imagine ridicule made triumphant
at the last minute
at the turn of a street
where you least expect it.

Kindness disguised as aloofness:
yet another strategy to mask
what lies beneath.

The carnivalesque is always a good
trustworthy guide for aimless
promenades where one pretends
to be made of steel.

Yet any good architecture
cannot resist fire. Sooner or later
the sustaining base will be apparent
the bricks will fall
the iron melt
the concrete dissolve

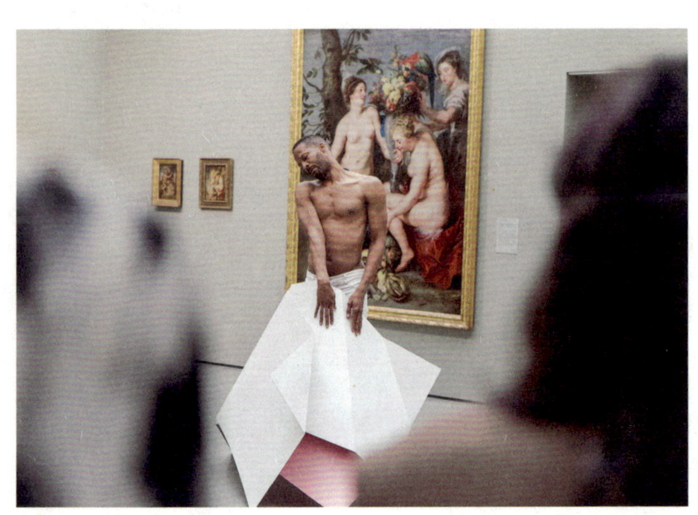

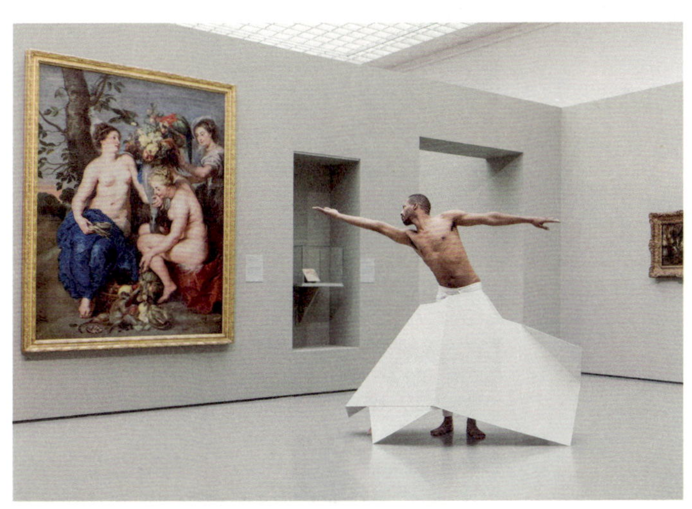

Metallica, 2018

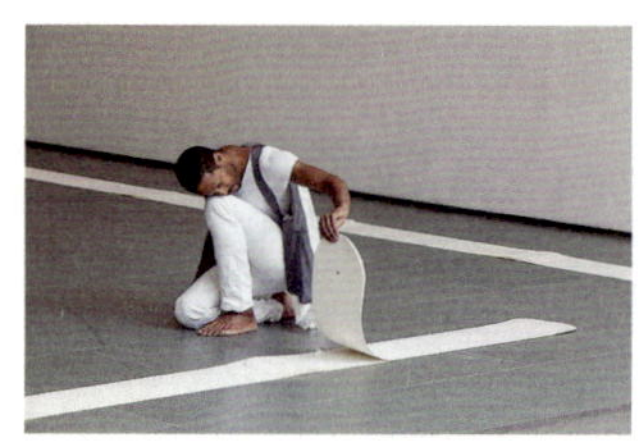

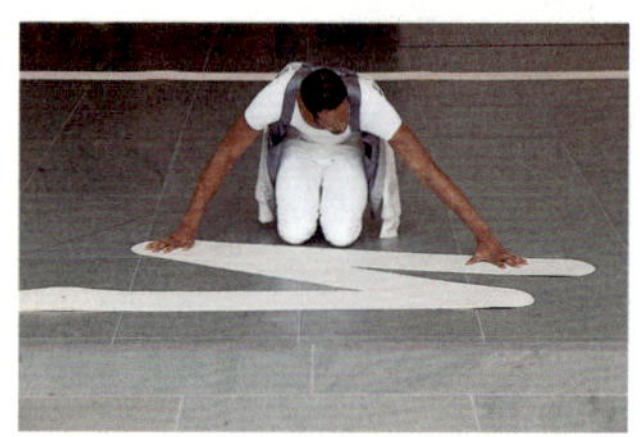

The Mile-Long Paper Walk (1965/2014), 2014

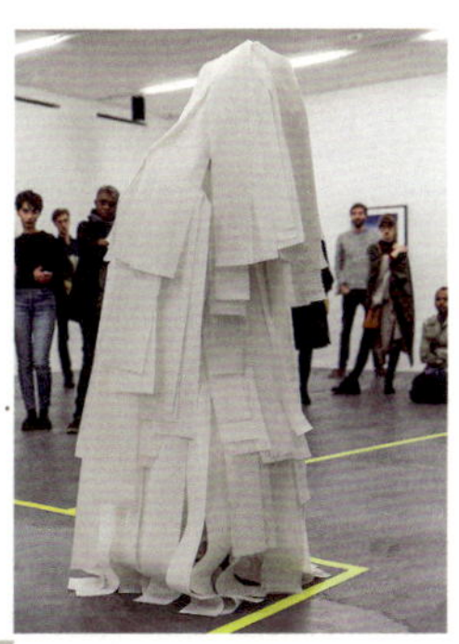

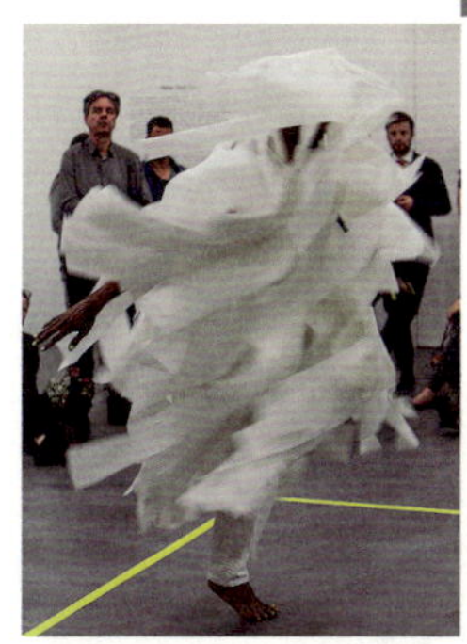

Abolibibelo, 2015

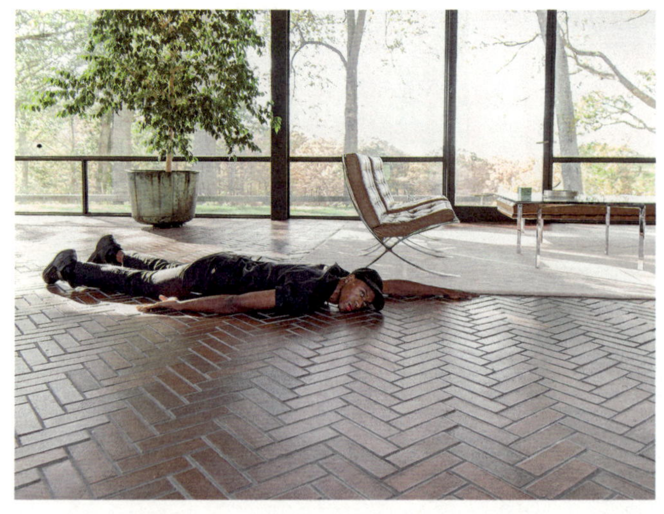

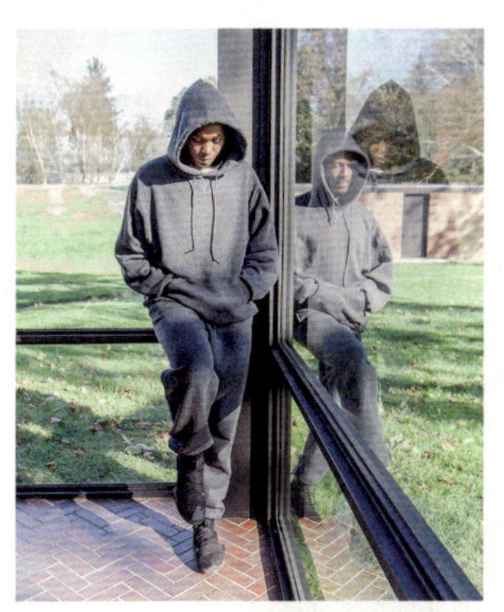

Imitation of Lives, 2017

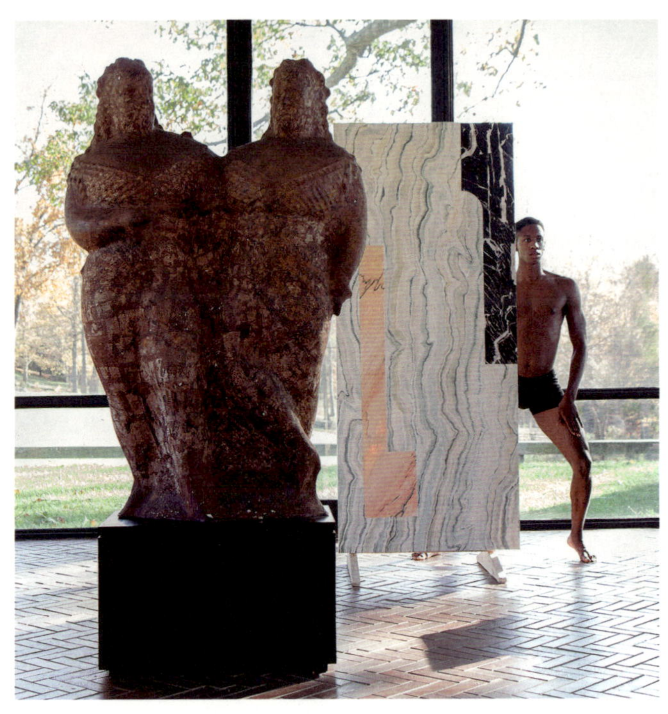

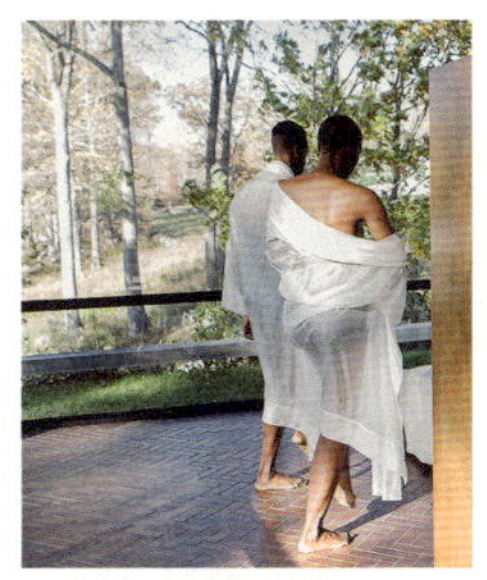

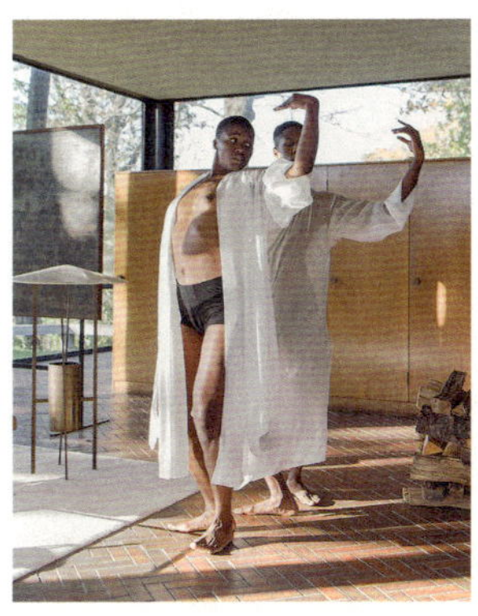

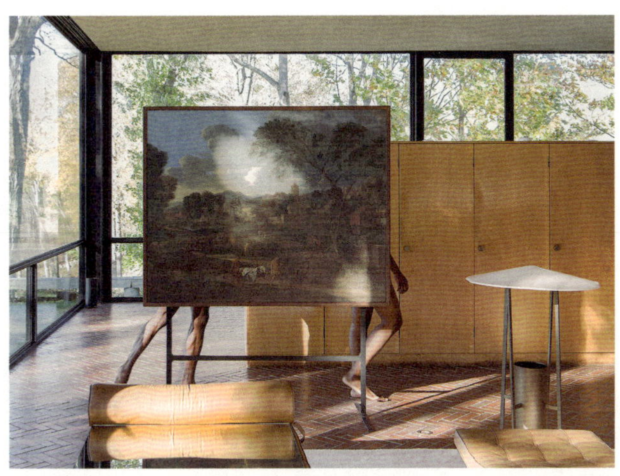

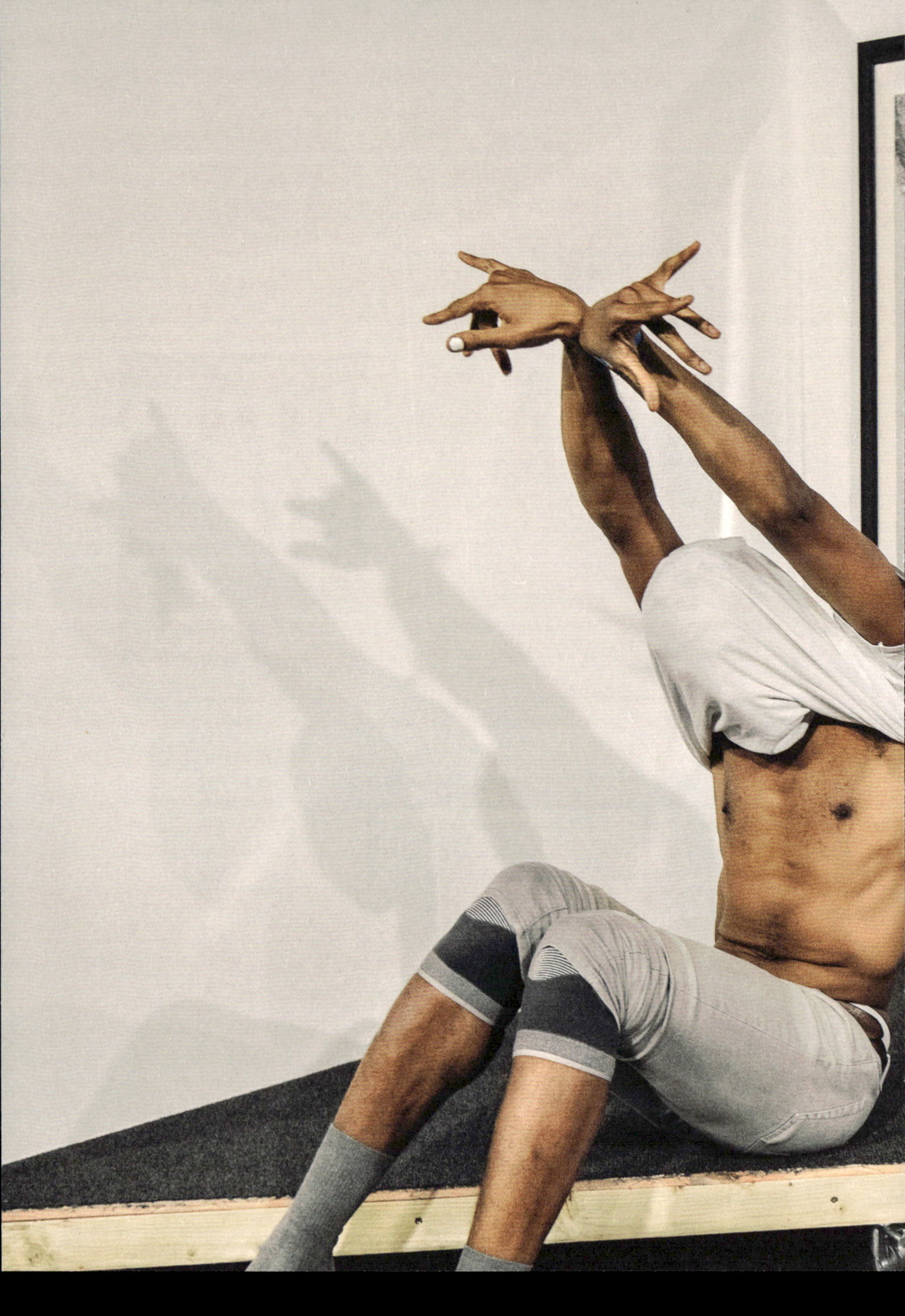

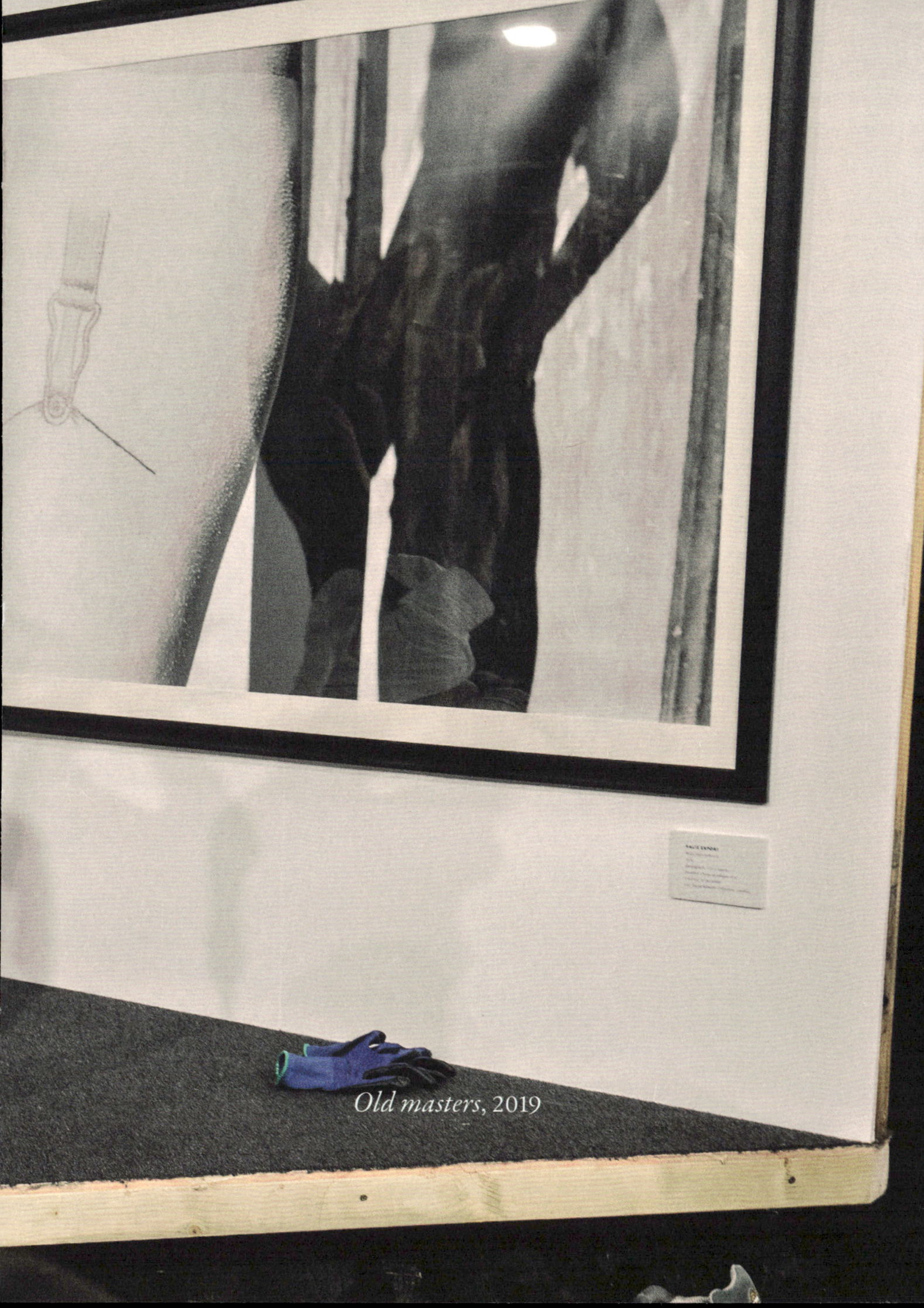

Old masters, 2019

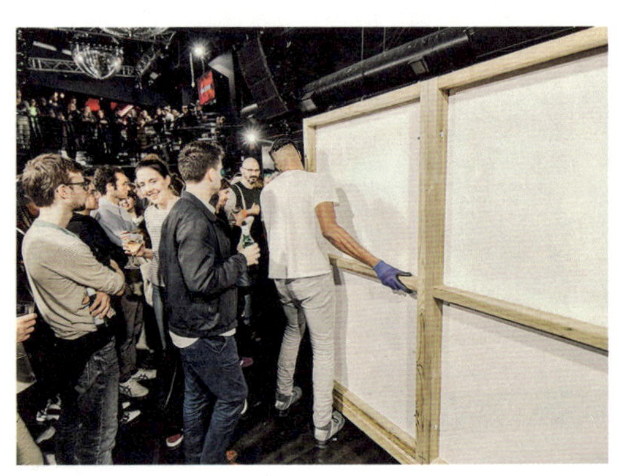

Old masters, 2019

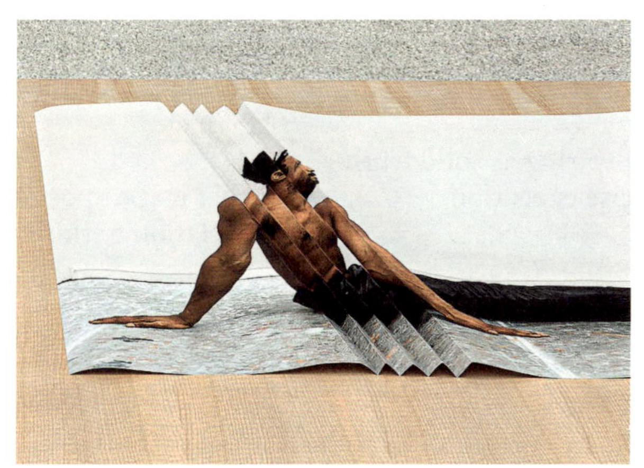

Plié I, 2020

Just as in language
Long legs, folded

Body disappearing under
its own weight
Not ballet but
the gravity

of porous materials
Skin
Paper

Transpiring as solid truth:
Precise execution

1, 2, 3 and again
plié

You get the jest?
What is your position
at this very moment?

Are you performing this
language?

What is your position
In relation to this text?

1, 2, 3 plié

Repeat the exercise
mechanically
until it is written all
over vour flesh
and bones

The body becomes
the word
on the paper

Again, plié

At one with the
image no body
yet a tender surface

To print
To pry

open

Plié (text), 2020

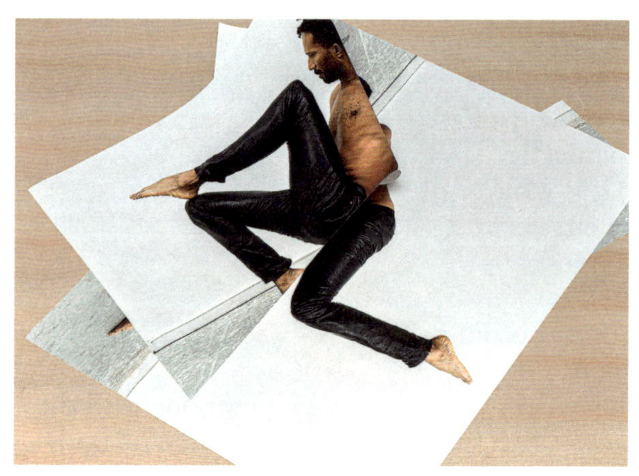

Plié IV, 2020

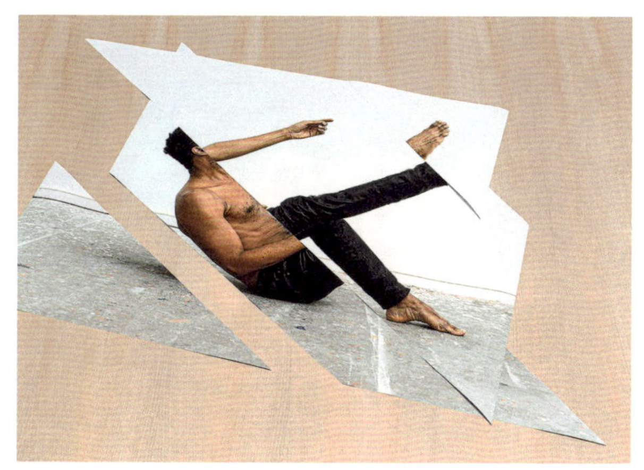

Plié III, 2020

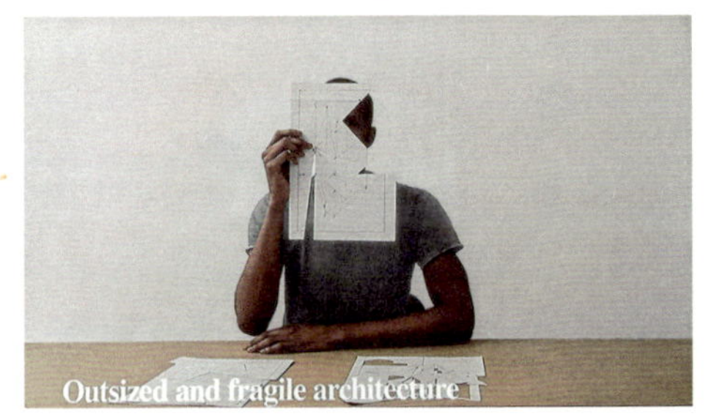

Paramètres, 2012

An Archive in the Head

A Conversation between
Kirsty Bell and Jimmy Robert

Kristy Bell In the twenty years that I've known you, you've lived in London, Brussels, Amsterdam, Berlin, Bucharest, and now you're about to move back to Paris. There is a myth that artists can work anywhere, but every artist needs a certain structure within which to work or things around them, even with a rather ephemeral practice like yours. Do specific places have a definitive influence on what you do?

Jimmy Robert I feel like movements always been part of my life. When I was really young, we moved to France from the Caribbean. My parents separated and I moved with my mom a lot in Paris and suburban Paris. So from very early on I had this idea of home being mobile and being different places. The only time that it was much harder was when I was around fifteen; we moved and I really missed my friends. I became a loner, I didn't socialize so much, I was listening to music and reading, in a total bubble. It closed things in. We had moved suddenly from a house into a flat, I shared the bedroom with my brothers so I didn't have space in which to explore. And that's maybe also what led me to leave home so early.

KB How aware of visual art were you at that time?

JR I don't think there was access to contemporary art—it was remote or distant. There was no real sense of it having a form of value or interest, or it being encouraged, simply because I think everything was about getting a job. There was a fear of creative things leading you astray. Very early on I was interested in ballet but my mum pushed it aside. But if something was prohibited or wrong, it would always be instantly interesting to me. When things were sanctioned or censored, it made me wonder, why?

I think my first approach to art came mostly through film or TV, rather than going to a museum. Museums happened later, when I was maybe seventeen. My philosophy teacher, who was a great influence, took us to the Musée d'Art Moderne in 1993 and that was the moment when I realized that ideas and art could be related. That art was not only illustrative, but that ideas could become objects, etcetera—there could be this transfer, this translation of things.

KB You began by studying literature at the Sorbonne. When did you realize it was not fulfilling your interests?

JR I think I did less than one semester of English literature at the Sorbonne. We were reading Chaucer and I thought, if I want to learn English, why not go to the UK, meet people, and be there where it's happening? I had met a boyfriend after finishing high school, at nineteen, and he lived in London so I was going back and forth already then. I was very much into indie pop music and in the early 90s everything was in London: fashion, music, drum and bass. I arrived and my partner was in a band and they were making music for Lea Anderson's dance companies, The Featherstonehaughs and The Cholmondeleys.

KB So you started seeing live dance performance at that young age in London?

JR I was already drawn to it since I had wanted to be a dancer and there were these people doing contemporary dance and physical theater all around me. I decided to continue doing English classes and in 1996 I did a BTEC as it was called at the time, an art foundation class, at Kingsway College. And there they told me to apply to Goldsmiths.

KB What kind of media were you were you drawn to then, in the mid-90s?

JR Photography and dance. I was looking at the work of Cindy Sherman, Sophie Calle, Christian Boltanski, also Annette Messager. These people were actually teaching at the Beaux-Arts in Paris, but I only discovered them when I had moved away. I remember very distinctly seeing an exhibition at the Pompidou in 1995 called *Feminin-Masculin, Le sexe de l'art*, with Louise Bourgeois, Niki de Saint Phalle, and Helen Chadwick, a lot of sculpture, and a lot of Cindy Sherman. It was exciting, seeing this work that questioned gender and sexuality. And physicality, sculpture, performance, different selves, the idea of framing. I remember running through the exhibition and thinking "Oh! Why didn't I see this before?"

KB Given your background in literature rather than visual media, was your approach to looking at art closer to an act of reading? Looking at an artwork as if it were a text and thinking about the frame, the relation to architecture, social aspects—so reading it in a broader context?

JR When I arrived at Goldsmiths I was supposed to write essays around art, and at the time it was all post-humanism, post-modernism, and all that. My first essay didn't fail, but it was close. I thought okay, I'm not invested in that, what can I do? I was more invested in Marguerite Duras, I was drawn to her writing, her style. Through reading *Hiroshima mon amour* and seeing it adapted into a movie—again, translation: novel to moving image.

I thought, I could write about this. So instead of writing about literature on a literature course at uni, I did it on an art course. My essays were always about literature or psychoanalysis.

KB You wanted to be a dancer but weren't allowed to be, so you found another kind of adjacency to dance. Then you were interested in literature but didn't want to be in that academic institution, so you came at it through another angle instead. To me that seems close to how your work developed and how it still operates: a sense of adjacency and looking at one format through another. The ways media can infect each other with their logic.

JR I started to look at Maurice Blanchot, Julia Kristeva, and their writings about writing. What it means to fill the paper with ink, to fill the empty space.

KB Is this what led you to work with paper as a central medium?

JR I was interested in the relation of language to the surface of the page. There were these really nice blue editions that were made in the 50s, Les Editions de Minuit, with a blue line around—a lot of Duras books were published by them. What I liked about them was their special paper. Sometimes you would have to cut the paper to open them, so there was a performative aspect.

And I like the intimacy of novel. You can take it with you, it's personal, it is physical, you touch it.

KB Did your interest in reading lead you to think in more conceptual terms? Looking beyond the words on the page at the structure, the support itself, the idea of what a book is, what literature is?

JR Yes, totally. Blanchot was very interesting because he was fundamentally questioning literature, the word, politics, the infinite, the finite. It was a playful and interesting way to think of the limits of material and then project that onto photography and say: okay, photography is supposed to represent, but what are the limits of its representational qualities?

KB Was that one of the primary questions that you were starting to formulate at that time?

JR The primary question was actually coming from philosophy, from a question we had in an exam: "Why desire the impossible?" That led me to think, okay, what do we aim for when we desire the impossible? It seems like a futile quest, but there is also a reason for it. It carries you through, keeps you going. And I thought that was easily applied to the idea of art and representation. There was also a philosophy class at high school called "Can man create?" about the whole idea of creativity—who created the world, where does it all come from? All these questions were poking at the core of things and forcing me to think: What can I do? What can art do? I think if I'd pursued other things, it would not have been so easy to approach these fundamental questions.

KB Does having a studio that is separate from your home affect your work? When did you have your first studio?

JR I was mostly working in my bedroom in London until I moved to Amsterdam for the Rijksakademie residency in 2004. That's the first time I had a studio. It was amazing. I realized, okay, I have this space, I should use it, make the most of it, and that meant expanding formats, trying things out, experimenting. It could become a rehearsal space: I would bring a carpet and warm up. Or I could experiment with more physical stuff. At the Rijks there was also money to live for the first time without having to work—not a lot of money, but it felt extremely luxurious. Especially after London, which was really tough. I was working most of the time—as an usher at the Lux Centre in Hoxton Square and at the Ritzy Cinema in Brixton—while making Super 8 films on my bedroom desk. There was very little time for other things. So coming to Amsterdam brought an explosion of possibilities. You not only had space but also a certain budget for production.

KB Is that when you started making photographic prints?

JR Yeah, I was making some already at Goldsmiths and experimenting with taking different kinds of papers through the printer, to see how the ink was sinking into the paper and bleeding. I did a lot of that at the Rijksakademie and started experimenting more with the idea of printing and sculpting, but writing also. My little book *Sweet Malady* was made there. It's about writing and reading and at the same time removing texts from legibility—it's all very influenced by Blanchot. Even the title is not readable and it opens like a leporello at the back, where there are various drawings about pages, paper: a kind of meta-box within a box. For me, these were ways of bringing the narrativity of form and the narrativity of content together into one object.

KB So in Amsterdam, all of those things were happening at the same time: performance, filmmaking, and working with paper, making books, writing?

JR Yeah, it created a basis for things. The stuff that I was already looking at when at Goldsmiths but didn't have the money or space to explore. I could expand it from the sketchbook into reality—there was finally time. I feel like this formed the basis of the things I'm still investigating now. There's still a lot of unresolved material.

KB When I look at the kind of works that you make, it's not obvious how to show them in an exhibition space. Works on paper, for instance, which are almost always shown without a frame, not behind glass. Or Super 8 film, which also poses a lot of questions around how to show it in an exhibition space.

JR Sometimes we show them on a projector, but they're so fragile, so sometimes they are digitized, or transferred onto 16 millimeter, which is a bit stronger. One has been transferred to 35mm. It was a Frieze Art Fair commission in 2006, together with Lux and Ian White, where several artists were invited to show films and videos in cinemas in London.

KB Which film of yours was transferred?

JR *L'Éducation Sentimentale*, a film about Bas Jan Ader. I was still in Amsterdam then and Bas Jan Ader had disappeared thirty years before. I asked my Dutch friend Bart van der Heide to play Bas Jan Ader because he's very tall. I didn't make it large on the screen because it was originally Super 8; I kept the image small with black space around it.

But to come back to the question about exhibition-making, I come to it from the angle that the image is not enough. It goes back to the idea of desiring the impossible and asking: What am I representing? Do I have the means to manage to represent something? And the image-object falls and fails at the same time.

KB So there is always an inadequacy, something that can't quite be complete?

JR Yeah, and that becomes a drive in itself. The fact that I know that I cannot complete the thing becomes a set of parameters for showing this inadequacy, the impossibility of completing or representing. Working from a lack becomes a way of making. Embracing that makes exhibition-making interesting. I do start with an intention, but I also believe that a lot of things will get in the way of that intention and transform it. And that it will become an interesting conversation, whether with the curator or the building itself.

KB That idea of conversation is palpable within the exhibitions, in the way the works react to each other. There isn't a sense of one piece just simply being separate and contained.

JR It's like wanting to have a conversation with the audience, between the works, with the curator, and making that manifest. The encounters with curators are the most interesting when there is a dynamic and we're responding to each other. That happened with Ian White because we were not only curator-artist, but also artist-artist. Collaborating with someone who will challenge you, and you challenge them back as well, forces you out of your comfort zone.

KB Your first collaboration with Ian White was the project *6 things we couldn't do but can do now* (2004), for which you learnt Yvonne Rainer's *Trio A* [1978]. It is interesting to think about that now in terms of your thwarted desire to be a dancer. You leapt into the medium again, from the outside. Ian was at that point primarily a curator and didn't identify himself as an artist, so you both crossed boundaries into areas that don't belong to you per se. Through accepting inadequacy, vulnerability, and imperfection, comes the possibility of transformation.

JR It was about learning to do a dance when you're not a trained dancer; a democratic dance that presumably anybody can learn, but that was actually quite difficult. We had to do a handstand and Ian had never done one, so he was really freaking out. We were training in the park and then he finally did it, and I was so happy. It was really challenging and crazy and stressful. We worked so hard, trying to master that piece, rolling over and over on the concrete floor because we didn't know any better, damaging our bodies in the process.

What was interesting about *6 things* and learning *Trio A* was the whole notion of what we couldn't do before but could do now. How having a studio and money from an institution enables you to do things—the practical economy. I had been approached by Catherine Wood to do something at Tate as part of their Art Now series and then worked with Ian to make this performance for it. We can do things when we are suddenly given some space and money, then we can learn, be aware. We can even become dancers for a moment.

In the same way, I am interested in using exhibition-making as something that allows you to do the things you want to do. I was approached once by a curator who asked if I would like to work with a choreographer. It was Kelly Kivland, she was at Bard [College] at the time, and through her I met Maria Hassabi, an artist and choreographer. Later Maria and I collaborated again: I asked her to direct me within my work. The work we made, *Counter-Relief* [2011], is made up of a film, a text, and some planks, and she could choreograph me with these objects and do whatever she wanted. She's into slow and sculptural movement, very different from what Ian and I did—it was an interesting way of learning another choreography.

KB In your collaborations with Ian White and Maria Hassabi, or in basing pieces on existing works by Bas Jan Ader or Yvonne Rainer, you approach the existing work or collaboration not as a reference but as a kind of prop or prompt. It is less appropriation, and more a kind of inhabitation of an existing form. That made me think about Sturtevant, how she was doing that and the very specific language she used, claiming that her process wasn't "copying" but "replicating." You were talking earlier about learning, and Sturtevant also talks about making replicas as a way to really understand the original works. This seems to occur in many instances in your work: understanding something through the process of activating it.

JR Yeah, learning and unlearning also, I would say. For example, with Yoko Ono's *Cut Piece* [1964], which I adapted for the performance *Figure de Style* [Cubitt, London, 2008], I was wearing a t-shirt made out of torn pieces of masking tape and reading aloud the reviews of how the Yoko Ono piece was interpreted by journalists at the time. Like you said, it's about learning, digesting, devouring. Also a positioning within art history—like, where am I in this? Once I'd gone from literature into art, my way of participating was to question art history and engage with it. It's funny you mention Sturtevant because she is in my show *Assymetrical Grammar*, at the Moderna Museet Malmö. I borrowed *Duchamp Fresh Widow* from the collection, which is a replica of Duchamp's *Fresh Widow*. Learning is the right term, I think. With *Trio A* it was the same: to embody. When Yvonne Rainer came in and corrected little details, it was as if we had become the material. It's a way of integrating the work into the body. But there is always a reason to firstly be drawn to certain work or artists and see them through my prism.

KB It's similar to what you were saying about being at Goldsmiths and writing about Marguerite Duras.

JR Exactly, there is the idea of the loop and circles and things coming back. What do we learn by repetition, by reproducing? You learn a song, the chorus, and it stays in your mind, and then you finally understand the lyrics.

KB That relates to this idea of performance practice and using the studio as a rehearsal space: rehearsal is just repetition, right?

JR And an exhibition is a try-out. Maybe it works, maybe it doesn't. Next time you will think about it differently. It is about embracing experiment and things not being set in stone.

KB Your recent survey show of twenty years of work travelled to three venues. Did you show the same works in each of those spaces?

JR Twenty years of different works in different spaces, each with different architecture. The exhibitions also each had different titles. *Akimbo* at Nottingham Contemporary [2020] focused more on language. In *Mirror Language* at the Museion in Bolzano [2021], the space itself was particular: there were no walls, so we had to build them. In *Appui, tendu, renversé* at CRAC Occitanie in Sète [2021], there was a series of rooms so we could really separate works and create different readings. And in *All dressed up and nowhere to go* at Kunsthalle Baden-Baden [2022]—the fourth exhibition, which was not part of the survey tour, but was somehow connected—it was more about the relation between performance and architecture. The exhibitions were looking at different works but not exclusively chronologically, so I don't think it felt like a survey. It was not attempting to create a story or a history. It was more about exhibiting these works in connection to each other and allowing them to say something, rather than creating the impression that they were somehow historical.

KB Were there things that surprised you about bringing together works that you made some fifteen or twenty years ago?

JR What surprised me, or what it highlighted, was rather a consistency of interest. I could see how something that didn't happen at a certain time happened later, because again, there was a situation, an opportunity, time, or space that enabled it. I could do the work at the Glass House [*Imitation of Lives*, Performa 17, 2017] because there was a performer who had been wanting to collaborate. But until there was an institution to invite me and pay my flight to New York, I couldn't make the work. And that took ten years!

KB Certain ideas exist in a holding pattern until there's an opportunity.

JR I see it also as a kind of library and an archive in the head, of things you would like to do. They're in the sketchbook or in some kind of mental box somewhere. I was visualizing doing something with General Idea's AIDS paintings, then the performance *Joie Noire* at KW [Institute of Contemporary Art] came up. I approached General Idea, but they wouldn't lend the *Black AIDS Painting*, so I had to find a strategy in order to include it. I ended up photographing my hand holding the book open at the page on which it was reproduced. So that's the same process, working within the limits of what you can and cannot do, where impossibility generates something.

KB Your body—or another person's body which becomes a kind of surrogate—forms a through-line in your practice, whether represented in film or photography, or as a live physical presence. I was thinking about how discourses around race, bodies, and public space have developed within that past twenty years, and particularly within the last five years, and wondered if this is something you consciously address in your work?

JR Yeah, I don't know. It's an interesting question. When I was at the 2022 Aichi Triennial, *Still Alive*, I had a brief conversation about this with curator Tobias Ostrander, about my 2008 performance *Figure de Style*. He was saying, "Coming from the US, we are past the idea of representation now because this discussion already happened." And I thought: well, it only just happened, we're not past it yet. This is just the beginning, it is not an end. If you think about gender and race in Japan, it's a whole different ballgame—many things are not even touched upon. When it comes to representation, so few women are in power and racism is fierce. So in a nutshell, it really depends where you are in the world and which perspective you have. A lot is up for question in Germany, France is another story again.

A lot is happening which is great, it's dynamic, but it's hard to generalize this movement and these ideas into a "now" that is transferable to everywhere. I think I can do it on a personal level and think about how to integrate these questions, or how to move on and simply think of another future, or of a moment that shifts to other concerns within the works.

KB When you performed *Figure de Style* at Cubitt in 2008, which I saw, the audience members were invited to pull a piece of tape off your skin—so touching your skin and even ripping out hair along the way. It was so demanding of intimacy from the audience and was almost as if the skin itself became a material.

JR I was also disturbed by it. I did it maybe twice after and then I thought, "I'm not doing this again." There was something about it that was really too much. There were moments when people grabbed the tape and it was really hard to take off and it was taking a hair off too. And I was asking myself, "Is that why I'm doing performance?" I didn't want to go into the direction of Marina Abramovic's durational performance. I veered away from work that I felt was also doing me personal harm.

KB It crosses over a threshold, with skin literally being a boundary.

JR Yeah. I once did a performance at Art Basel where I was projecting a film on my naked back [*Object/My Affection*, 2007]. It suddenly struck me as I was doing it that I was actually objectifying or commodifying myself in a way that I didn't want. There was a director of some institution who came and was just looking at me naked, you know—it was not about looking at the work. I realized I was producing something that was almost the opposite of my intent.

KB In your work there is the experimenting and process and learning, but also a structure underlying that. It feels rigorous.

JR In performance, dancers also have rigor, they are disciplined. Even if it looks like somebody is just moving around, they've rehearsed, they've practiced that. Ian White wrote about this and I quote him in the booklet for *Imitation of Lives*, about the actor repeating the same movement each time. Where it feels like the movement just happened in the film, but it was actually rehearsed and practiced. This idea of liveness in its different aspects was something he was really interested in. I think about the idea of liveness between performance and photography, which is also influenced by stillness versus liveness. Breathing life into sculptures, interrupting them, or more complex interactions.

KB There is a distinct lightness and delicacy in your exhibition-making and in your performance, but the density of thought that allows your works to appear light is anything but accidental.

JR Sometimes I want things to be a bit messier, but structure always comes back—not as a safety net, but maybe as a way of finding a formal composition. However much I try to be messy, I never really manage.

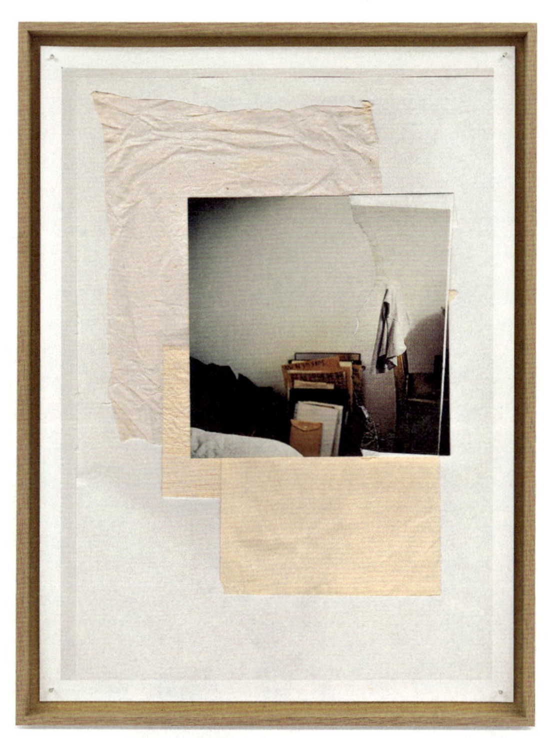

Untitled (Desk), 2013

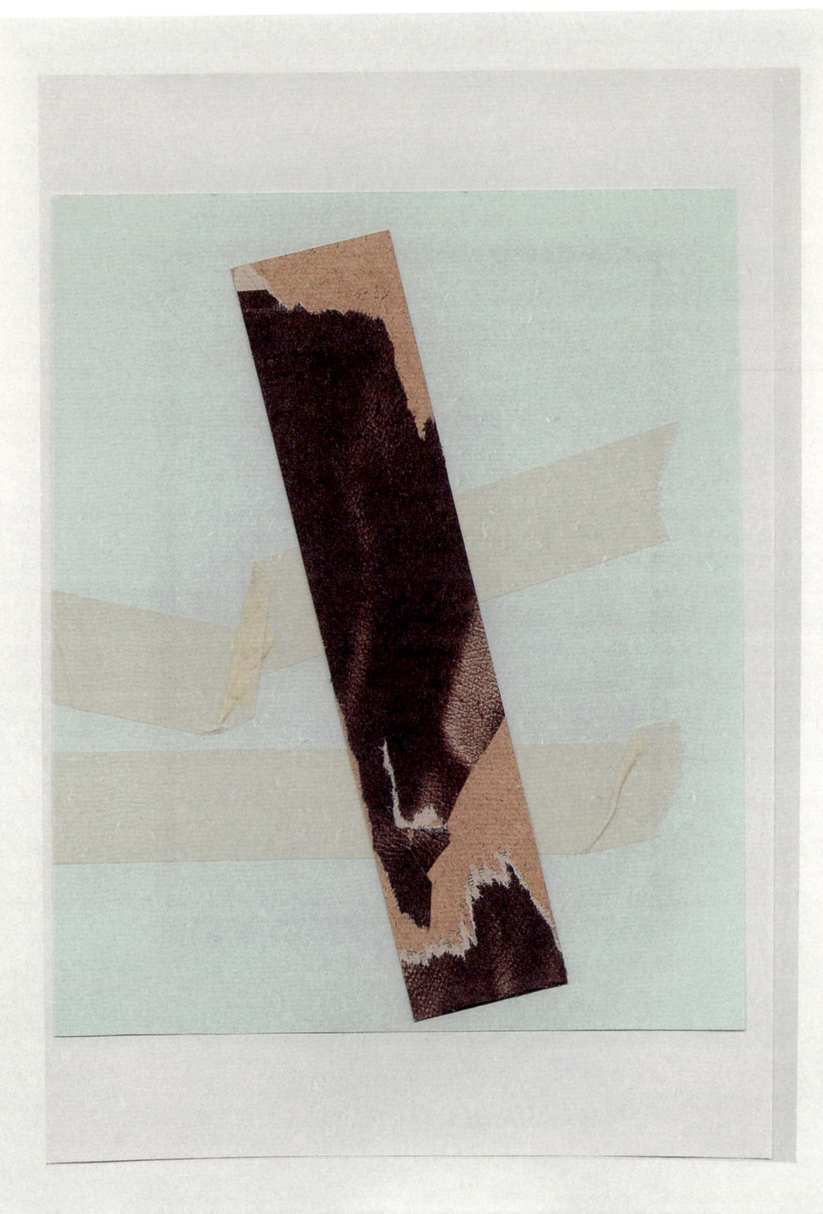

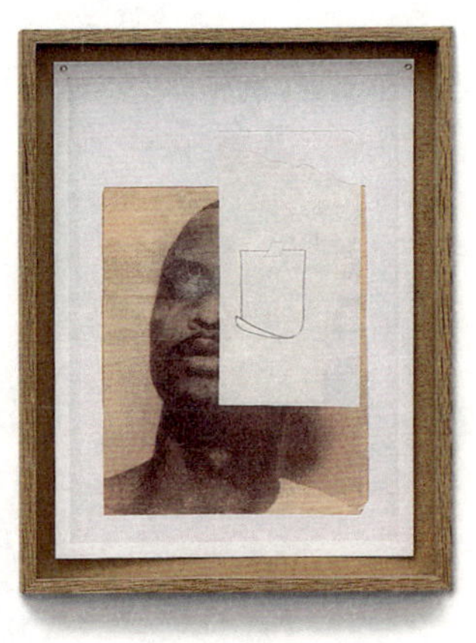

Untitled (Skin/Visage), 2013

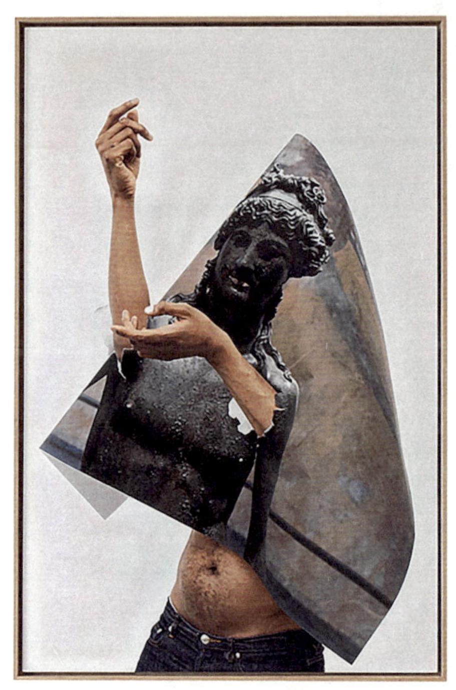

Frammenti VII, 2022

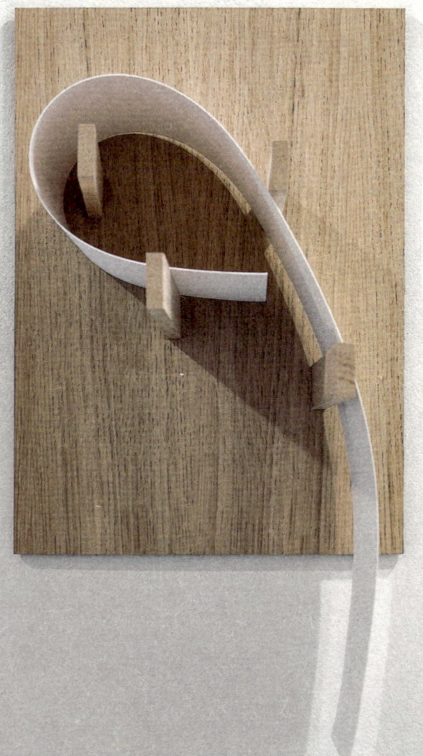

Untitled (Patterns), 2018

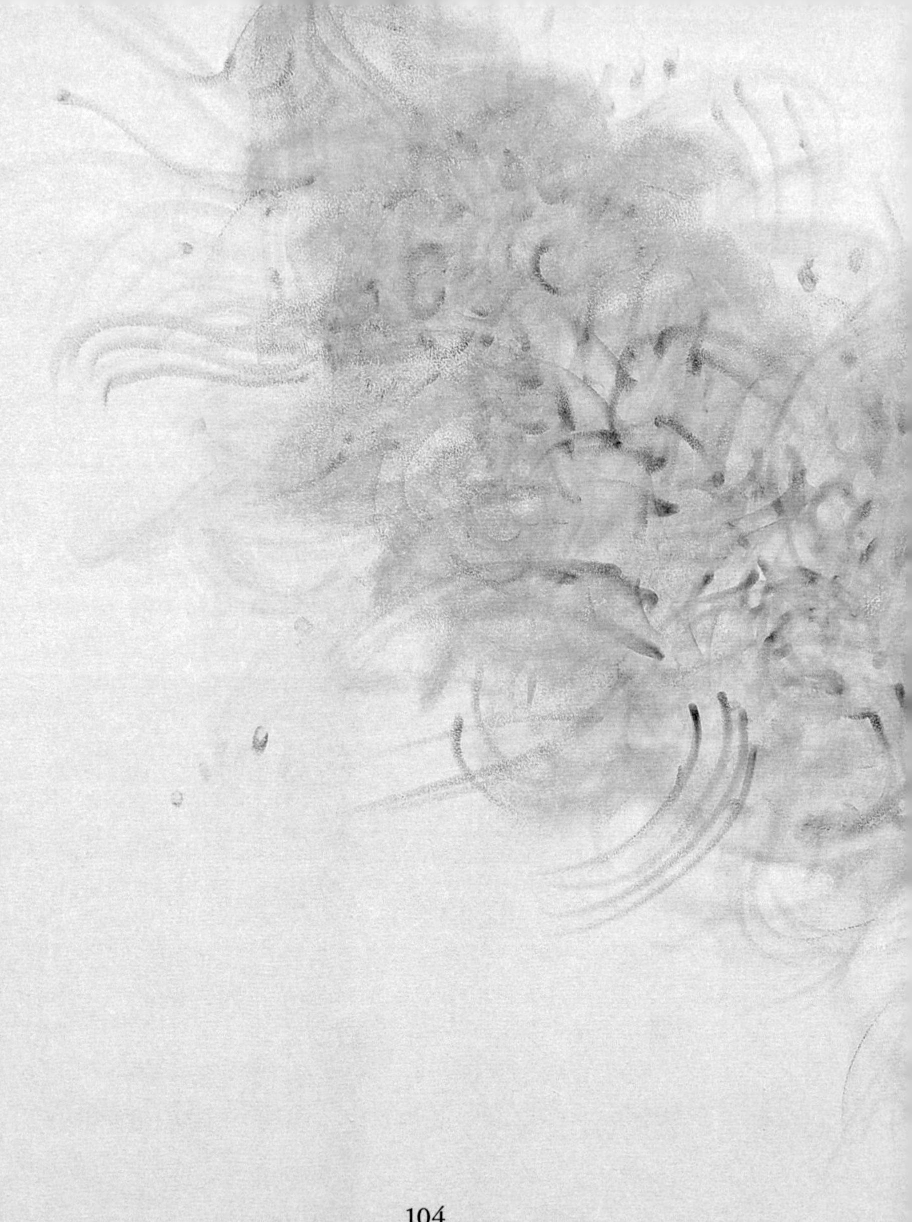

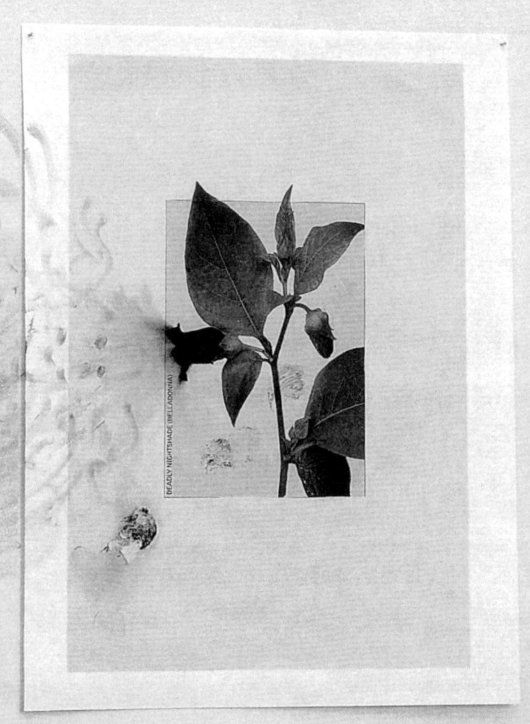

Untitled (Belladonna), 2007/2021

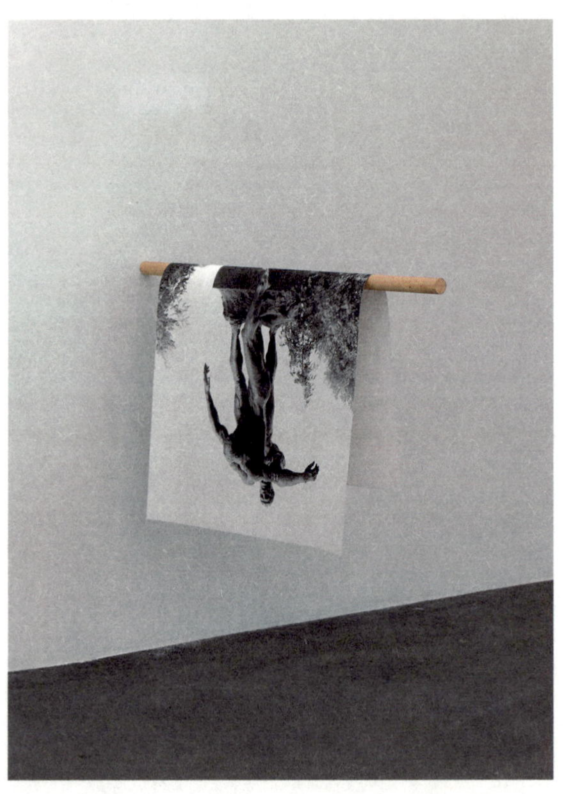

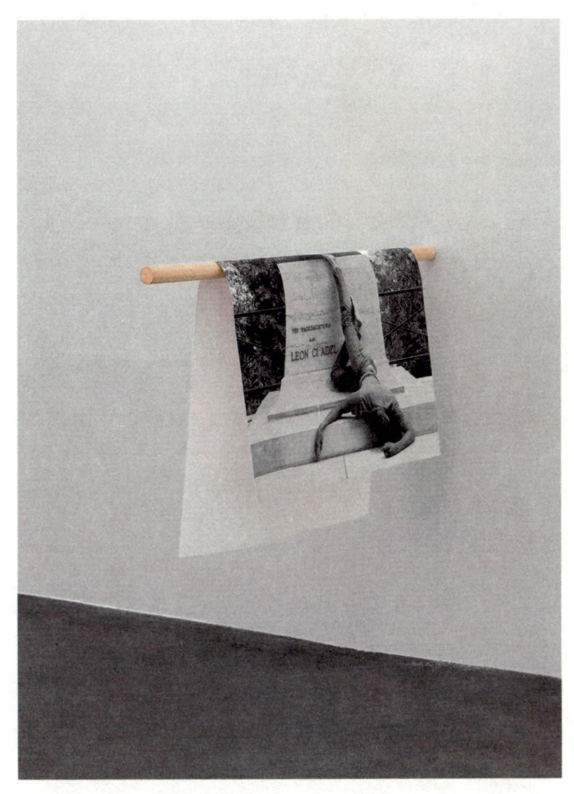

Untitled (Ompdrailles), 2013

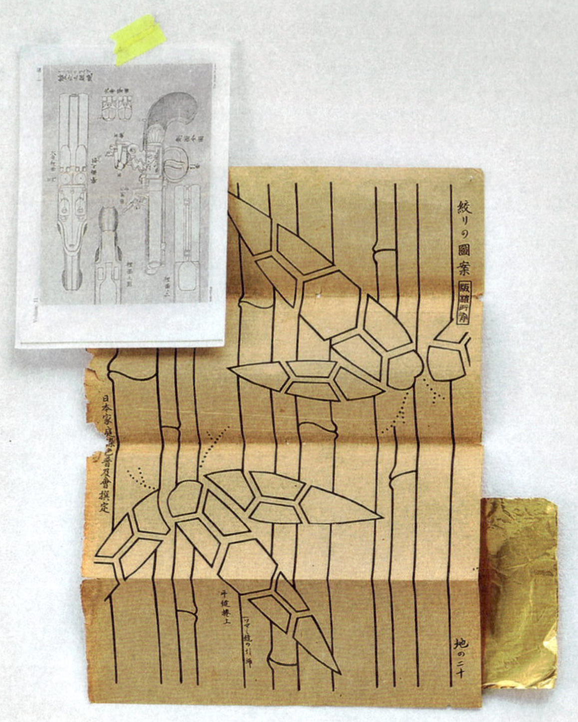

Technique et Sentiment II, 2021

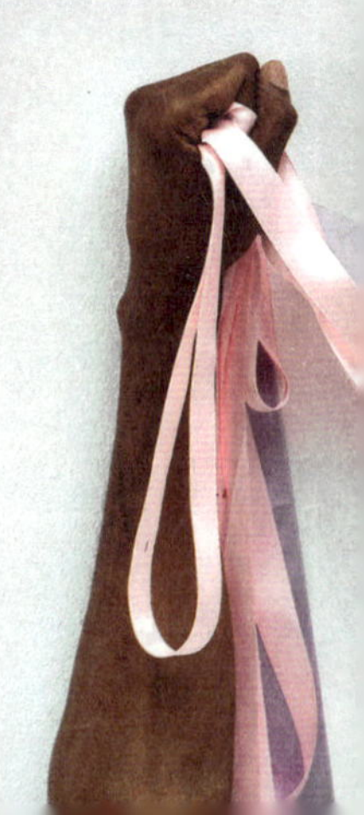

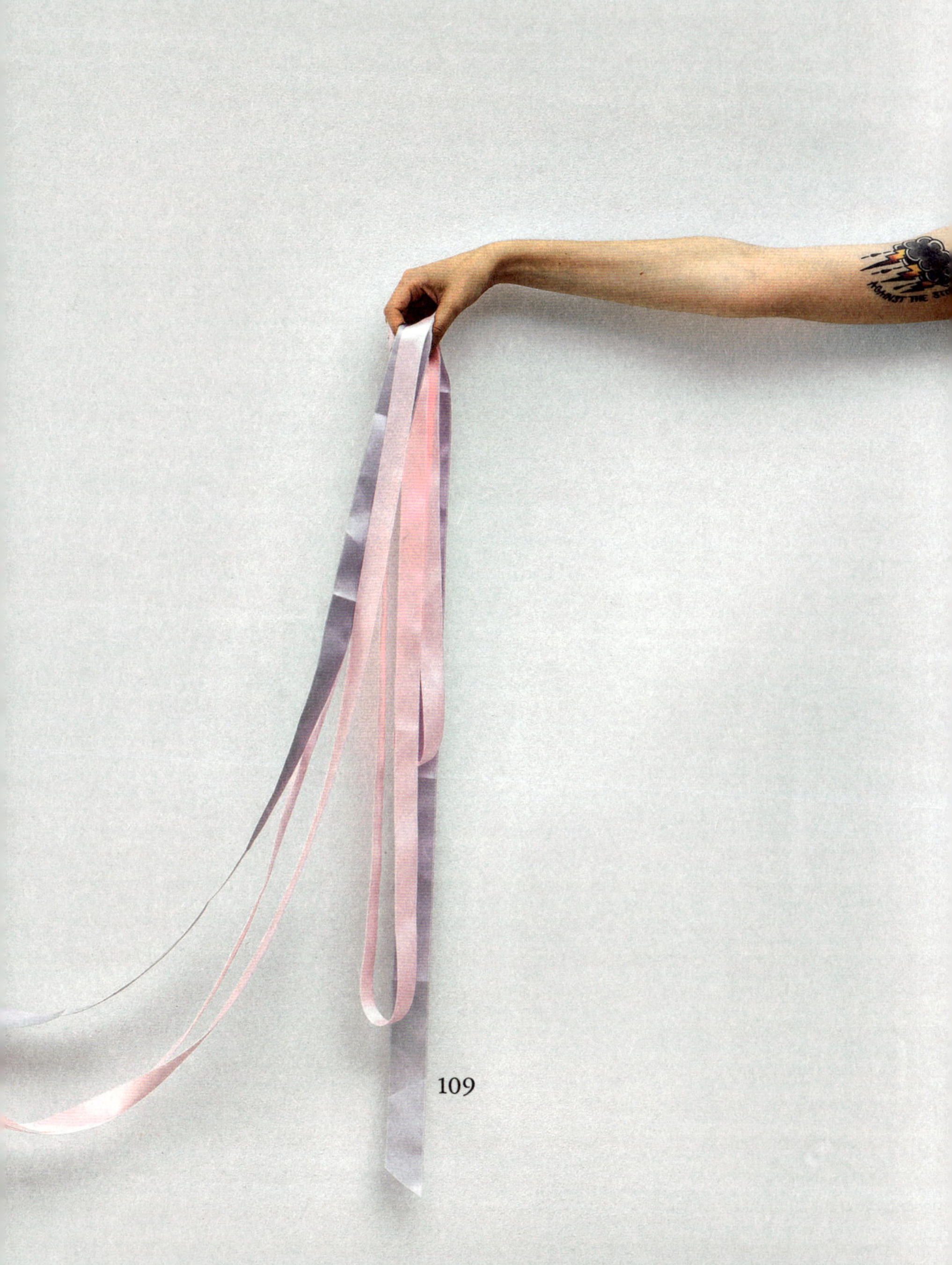

set up the parameters
adjust the structure

define the place one speaks from
who speaks? In the name of whom?
data, insignificant calculations
these measurements appease or unnerve

bail out of formatted minds
distinguish the limit from the edge
the dubious scientific approach
unsettle the apparatuses, question them even
base line of deformed minds

a direction or another wouldn't be inconsequential
titillated by verbal feats
while hiding behind an oblique language

set up the parameters
adjust the structure

static shots and elevations
the form of the text coerces the movements
however free they regarded themselves
liberated from all technique

the dimension you evolve in
is it a pose or posturing?

outsized and fragile architecture
of a seductive yet redundant reported speech
troubadours and trinkets generate
pleasant linguistic asymmetries

how could I imagine that our bodies
would be made to measure even?

set up the parameters
Adjust the structure

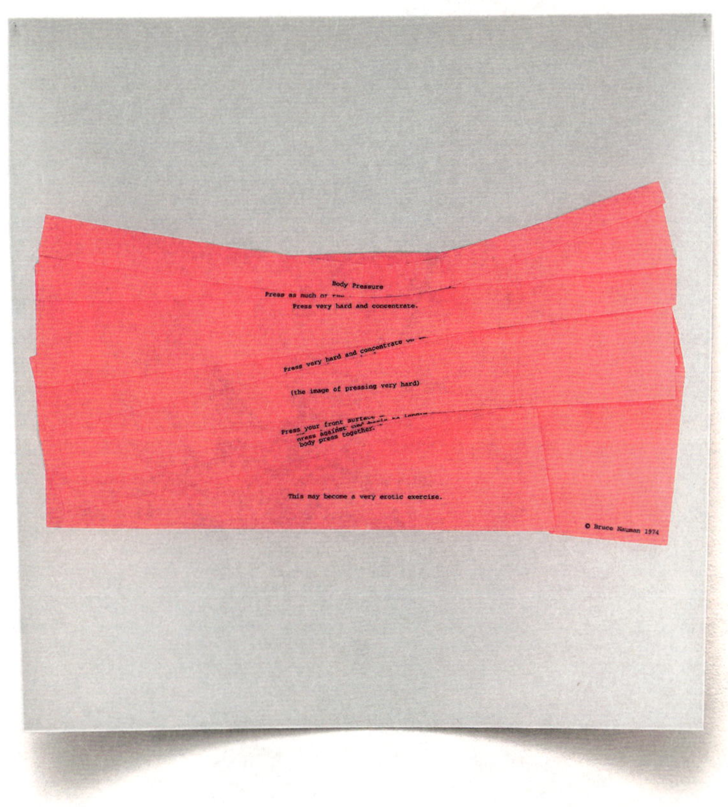

Cadavre exquis, 2010

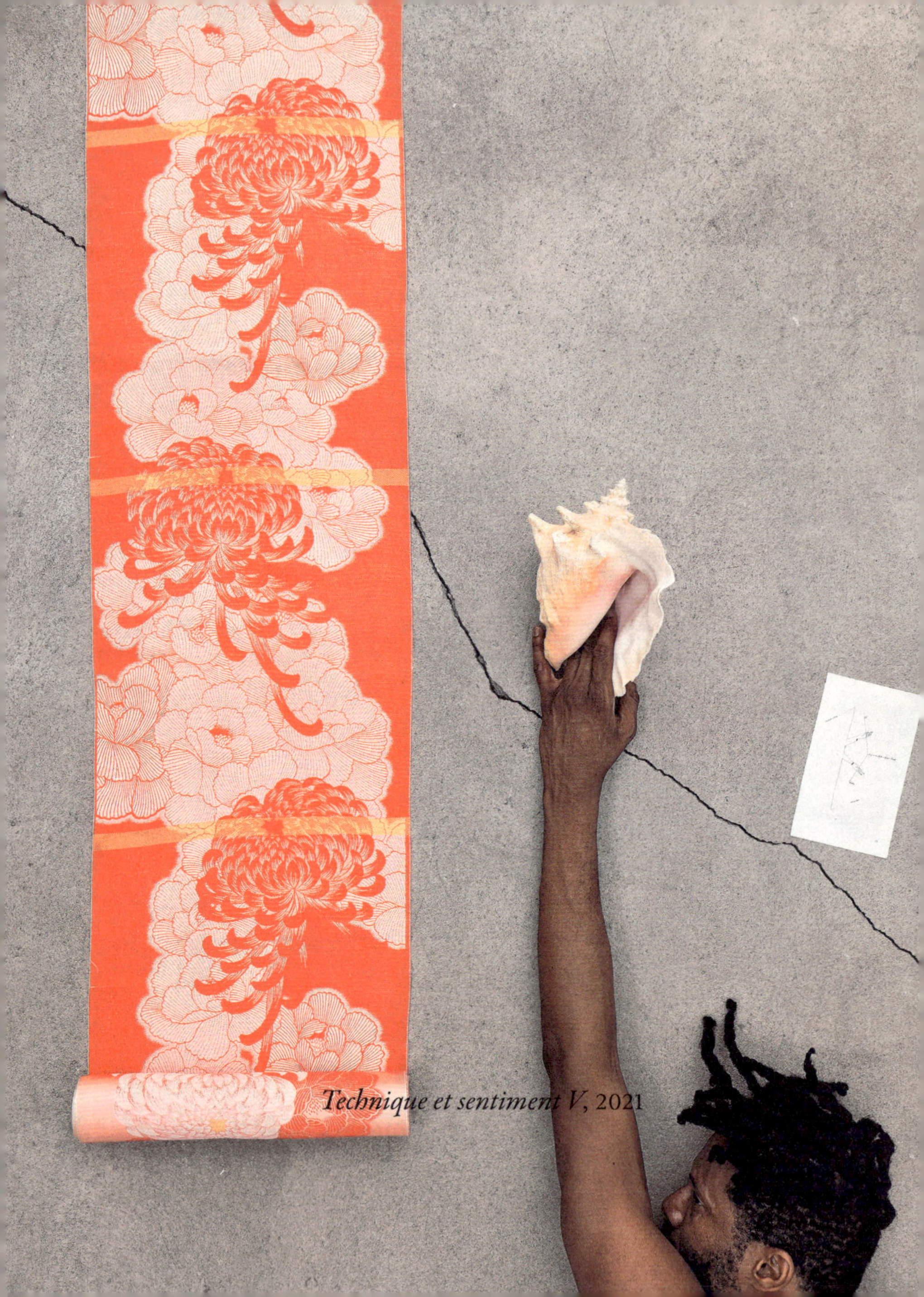

Technique et sentiment V, 2021

While descending.

Elisabeth Lebovici

"Did I descend it well?" The little phrase has been running through my head. They say that at the Casino de Paris in 1933, Cécile Sorel shouted it out during the gala evening for the first "Vive Paris" variety show. Cécile Sorel, a member of the Comédie-Française, was then sixty years old, a fairly advanced age to be making a music-hall debut. For the ex-actress, recycled as a fledgling variety show captain, it was a major challenge to descend the stairs of the music-hall set without falling flat on her face with its haughty expression. Once she had reached the foot of the Casino's 100-step staircase, she called those words to Mistinguett—herself also a cheeky sixty-year-old—who was only waiting for a misstep from her old friend who was less experienced in the trade. Sorel got nothing in return for her question; it brooked no answer. "Did I descend it well?" Usually descent does not have a positive evaluation tied to it. Descent into hell, descent upon a target, descent into madness, descent from the cross... A descent is never done *well*. And yet maybe it would be enough to shift its temporality slightly, to go back in time somewhat, to stop it in the act, to suspend it when it takes place. In order to name this *choreographic* moment, let us use an unknown French gerund: *descendance*. Let us effect a displacement in language, from the noun (*une descendance*) to the verb (*en descendance*), drifting between what the two suggest: one defines its identity, while the other impresses a performative, and the interaction suspends both of them. Let us move towards an act that articulates the silent dialogue between two old actresses waiting for the chance to catch each other out, while one of them is in the process of inventing herself a new body. Phonetically, *descendance* is not far from *dissidence*.

Descendance also means having an alternative kind of *l'esprit d'escalier* (literally "staircase wit"), even if at this point Josephine Baker has to take Cécile Sorel's place on the staircase. Before triumphantly descending the stairs of the Folies-Bergère or the Casino de Paris, Baker knew how to perfectly incarnate what the primitivist codes of exoticism expected from an "African" performer when the fad for Black American music and dance was at its peak. Her "Danse sauvage" in the *Revue Nègre* (1925) exemplified it. But Josephine Baker, with her grimacing pantomime, knew just as well how to reverse this fetishism and turn it into a process of emancipation by incorporating the cultural codes of her Empire audience into her body movements, her costumes, her songs

("I have two loves"), her house,[1] and her social life offstage. From the racialized ghost to the elegant starlet, she mastered the imaginative geographies encoding her identity (naked Africa, America's march to mechanization, colonial France), in order to better make them into parodist subjects.[2] This is called the decolonization of a body. Sowing total confusion between what could appear authentic, original, and what seemed like pure invention, Josephine Baker created for herself an "entirely fictional, elastic ethnicity,"[3] a cosmopolitan one: an oblique figure. Back to the staircase.

In my view, this is also what kindles the relationship between the title of the exhibition in Delme, *Descendance*, and what it exhibits.[4] The staircase is indeed there, but it is not climbed or descended. Concerting voices come from above, but one cannot go find them. And the staircase finds itself set up in the exhibition as a scale model. It is

1 Baker enlisted the services of Viennese modernist Adolf Loos to design her house in 1928.

2 Jean-François Staszak, "Performing Race and Gender: The Exoticization of Josephine Baker and Anna May Wong," *Gender, Place and Culture* 22, 5 (2015): 626–64.

3 Terri Francis, "Embodied Fictions, Melancholy Migrations: Josephine Baker's Cinematic Celebrity" in Jeremy Braddock and Jonathan P. Eburne (eds.), *Paris, Capital of the Black Atlantic: Literature, Modernity, and Diaspora* (John Hopkins University Press, 2013), 138.

4 Jimmy Robert, *Descendances du nu (Descendance of the Nude)*, Centre d'art contemporain - la synagogue de Delme, June 18–September 25, 2016.

a geometric shape, an element spilled onto the floor. Or a mask, a performance leftover. I am thinking of Oskar Schlemmer's characters and mobile architectures. I am also thinking of those famous architects dressed up as skyscrapers for the 1933 Beaux-Arts Ball in New York. I am thinking of the Dada mask and tubes worn by Sophie Taeuber during her abstract dances at Zurich's Cabaret Voltaire in 1917. The mask, which was only seen in the performance (it later disappeared) made it possible to give free rein to spontaneous movements in "points and ridges," in which "lines broke against her body."[5] And since Sophie Taeuber was a teacher at the School of Applied Arts in Zurich, the mask also made it possible to hide her face and free herself from professional retribution. The mask's face-double is also what the great psychiatrist and anticolonial activist Frantz Fanon described: a melancholic and flamboyant strategy.

The series of last paintings made by Marcel Duchamp in 1911–12, entitled *Nude Descending a Staircase*,[6] caused a scandal and was rejected by viewers and critics alike.

5 Hugo Ball, *Über Okkultismus, Hieratik und andere schöne Dinge* (Surkamp, 1984), 56–7.

6 Three known versions are held by the Philadelphia Museum of Art: (1) Marcel Duchamp, *Nude Descending a Staircase (no. 1)*, 1911, oil on cardboard on panel; (2) Marcel Duchamp, *Nude Descending a Staircase (no. 2)*, 1912, oil on canvas, the best known; (3) Marcel Duchamp, *Nude Descending a Staircase (no. 3)*, 1916, graphite, pen and black ink, black paint, colored pencil or crayon, and blue wash on gelatin silver photograph.

One critic characterized the no. 2 of the series as "an explosion in a shingle factory," which would have been welcome had it not been pejorative. It is often said that in these paintings Duchamp was exploring the problems faced by classical representation with the arrival of mechanical reproduction techniques like chronophotography and the advent of cinema (and cinema, under the names *Papitou*, *Zou-Zou*, and *Princess Tam-Tam*, was featuring Josephine Baker).[7] Like a kind of mechanical choreography, it represents positions. The displacement of the nude is an abstraction. Duchamp said: "The movement of form in time inevitably ushered us into geometry and mathematics."[8] This observation leads to a point where movement disappears completely, giving way to a ghost. The one that keeps a nude waiting. This nude—since the nineteenth century, and in the bourgeois tradition of Western representation—has primarily been the reification of a female body in a few poses,[9] even if the title of the painting omits its gender and leaves it up to grammar, which declines it in the masculine in French.

7 She is Papitou of the Antilles in *Siren of the Tropics* (1927), Zou-Zou in the eponymous film of 1934, and represents all of the French colonies in *Princess Tam-Tam* (1935).

8 Duchamp, quoted by Pierre Cabanne, *Dialogues with Marcel Duchamp*, trans. Ron Padgett (Da Capo Press 1987), 31.

9 Sandra Bartky, *Femininity and Domination: Studies in the Phenomenology of Oppression* (Routledge, 1990), 63–82.

Here, the anatomy's stratification into chips with "the harsh colour of wood"[10] transmutes into the soft folds of a curtain. Broken up into a decorative motif, repeated by varying the orientations, and emphasized by circular and square lines, the Nude and the Staircase enter into a new morphology, endowed with a new, exciting, diasporic body, transferred onto the moving, continuous material of the curtain. The ghost, hiding behind the mask of the imitation-wood paint, reveals itself in the texture, whose various brown tones give visibility to skin colors, yellows, beiges, chestnut, and browns. Calling oneself brown or feeling brown means formulating an "apparatus that permits us to read ethnicity as a historical formation uncircumscribed by the boundaries of conventional understandings of identity."[11] For queer theorist José Esteban Muñoz, who set out the notion, feeling brown means feeling emotions, experiencing the affects of a minority aesthetic, in which the practices of people who are neither heteronormative nor white become visible. On the surface of the skin.

In recent years, this has been designated by the term "intersectionality," coined in the late 1980s by jurist

10 Duchamp, quoted in Dalia Judovitz, *Déplier Duchamp : passages de l'art* (Presses du Septentrion, 2000), 29.

11 José Esteban Muñoz, "Feeling Brown: Ethnicity and Affect in Ricardo Bracho's The Sweetest Hangover (and Other STDs)," *Theatre Journal* 52, 1 (2000): 67–79.

Kimberlé Williams Crenshaw.[12] It defines not multiculturalism, but rather the meeting, intersection, entanglement, and connections between identity and gender, racial identity and class identity for example, establishing a complex locus where privileges and oppressions meet. These problems have long been explored by Black feminist lesbian writers like Audre Lorde, or Chicana writers like Gloria Anzaldúa and Cherríe Moraga.[13] Both of the latter have celebrated the cultural interweaving and ambiguous contradictions of miscegenation (*meztizaje*) as an absolute margin and the center of a multifarious subjectivity. "Brown bodies are those bodies that break away from the expectation of whiteness as the norm," writes Salvador Vidal-Ortiz. "Yet Brown bodies are also queered in that they are seen as suspicious, as already delinquent, especially in relation to immigration but also to not fully participating in U.S. citizenry."[14] This is painfully reminiscent of the current situation in Europe, particularly in France and Belgium.

12 See Kimberlé Crenshaw, "Mapping the Margins: Intersectionality, Identity Politics, and Violence against Women of Color," *Stanford Law Review* 43, 6 (1991): 1241–99.

13 Gloria Anzaldúa, *Borderlands/La Frontera* (1981) and Cherrie Moraga and Gloria Anzaldúa (eds.), *This Bridge Called My Back: Writings by Radical Women of Color* (Persephone Press, 1981).

14 Salvador Vidal-Ortiz, "Introduction," in Vidal-Ortiz et al. (eds.), *Queer Brown Voices: Personal Narratives of Latina/o LGBT Activism* (University of Texas Press), 14–15.

What happens in practice when the Black/white, interiority/exteriority, and essence/mask binary systems fail on the surface of the skin? Let us conduct the experiment on that multiplicity of browns which invade and transform one of Sherrie Levine's woodcuts, *After Duchamp*. This was part of the series *Meltdown* (1989). Once again, an action performed *en descendance*. It consists of four woodcuts made on Japanese rice paper, a traditional process combined in this case with a computer's digital resources.[15] Making up a grid of twelve rectangles (3 × 4), they are digital reductions of reproductions of paintings that were scanned and, using a graphic application, transformed into twelve pixels, which determined each of the monochrome rectangles. The color of each pixel is itself derived from a medium tone, losing all of the chromatic events that might have been found in the "original" reproduction. When one learns that the Duchamp painting which served as the guinea pig for this digital treatment was *LHOOQ* (1919)—an *assisted readymade*, that is to say the addition of a painted moustache to a photo of the *Mona Lisa*—extra complexity is added to this network of transitions at play between means of production and reproduction, literally causing a shift from one gender to another. Continuing this network of transitions "after

15 In addition to *After Duchamp*, the set of woodcuts includes: *After Monet*, *After Kirchner*, and *After Mondrian* (Peter Blum Editions, 1989).

Sherrie Levine," Jimmy Robert adds a turn of the screw by transferring the *LHOOQ* process to *Nude Descending a Staircase II* and its brown tones. How can justice be done to all the elements that come into the composition of the arts? Maybe it starts with getting to the surface of the skin of hidden stories, stories of bodies, which regain visibility in a digital dissolution.

Arriving home one evening at dusk, Vassily Kandinsky encountered a mysterious, "indescribably beautiful picture" that he did not recognize. It was one of his own paintings, on its side against a wall in the shadow of nightfall. "Now I could see that objects harmed my pictures,"[16] he decided. In his self-justifying narrative, he forgot its creator, with whom he did not identify. The abstraction caused a *machination*. Writer Alain Robbe-Grillet, in his film *Eden and After* (1970), also experimented with that oblique transition from one position to another. A painting becomes figurative, its geometric shapes sketching a view of a house and water on Djerba Island (Tunisia), as photographed on a postcard; or conversely, shifting the horizontal and the vertical, he moves towards abstraction, going from the blue sea and the exotic view to the wall of a student's bedroom. The painting causes the film to transition from one space to another, like in David Lynch's *Mulholland Drive* (2001),

16 Vassily Kandinsky, *Complete Writings on Art* (G. K. Hall & Co., 1982), 369–70.

in which a blue box transposes the two female characters from one world to another parallel world that is just as realistic and troubling, or like Jacques Rivette's *Celine and Julie Go Boating* (1974), in which magic candy causes transitions from one narrative to another. Or like Louise Lawler in her photographic works, in which *White Flag* by Jasper Johns—hanging over the bed of a couple of collectors (to take one of her many examples, which are always particular)—triggers a similar transition from one narrative to another that is just as strange and familiar.

In Jimmy Robert's exhibition, in the large photograph of two white walls (one imagines picture rails, on which Delme can be easily projected), one sees a painting turned on its side and propped against a wall. It seems somewhat cut off by the angle of the wall closest to the front, but one can make out its resemblance to Sturtevant's photographic collage *Nude Descending a Staircase* (1996). This itself recasts her 1968 film *Duchamp Nue Descendant un Escalier. Descendance* is feminized. There is also Gerhard Richter, whose *Ema (Akt auf einer Treppe)* (1966) uses paint to blur a frontal photograph of a white, nude woman descending a grey-brown staircase. Familial and patriarchal intimism (it is apparently a painting of his wife on the staircase leading to his studio) substitutes for the experimental verification of a set of instructions. It is only half-surprising that the German title of *Ema (Nude on a Staircase)* stayed in the masculine. The masculine, in fact, seems always to be the gender of the perspective that beholds it (even if it is that of a woman) and not that of the body which this perspective beholds. But this is not the case for *Nude Descending a Staircase*. When the image substitutes for Richter's painting, it shifts towards another gender. A female nude immediately becomes a bit more undressed, in terms of the distinction—made by cultural historian John Berger after historian Kenneth Clark—between two words: nude and naked. "To be nude is to be seen naked by others and yet not recognized for oneself [...] To be naked is to be oneself. [...] Nudity is placed on display. [...] The nude is condemned to never being naked. Nudity is a form of dress."[17] Like Josephine Baker, the Nude in Sturtevant's work becomes object and subject, active and passive. The arrangement of the photograms stratifies the image like stair steps, and this operation revives the conceptual process that makes "artistic representation function like a collection, a system of assembly and labelling."[18] Through this translation, it is the image that in reality *relives* the making of a creative activity without any creative act—a reproduction machine; the image does not measure a reproduction's supposed faithfulness to the original. Following this logic, its new photographic translation in Delme shows it to us in a situation. By propping it against a wall, like a Richter

17 John Berger, *Ways of Seeing* (BBC and Penguin Books, 1972), 54.
18 Dalia Judovitz op. cit., 13.

painting taken off its picture rail, the panel "after Louise Lawler" exhibits the circulation system through which every art object constructs its history. It is not limited to conceptual operations and fabrication techniques. It continues well beyond these, passing from hand to hand, from wall to wall, and from context to context, through exhibition circumstances, through the proliferation of reproductions, through marketing or restoration, through the visibility of the object in question or its withdrawal and disappearance, through its integrity or its ruin. Its history is also that of this *descendance*. Descending the staircase also means taking the nude off its pedestal, carrying it towards its diasporic destiny.

Postcript.

Years have passed since the writing of this text, impulsed by and for Jimmy Robert's *Descendances du nu* (2016) exhibition and eponymous performance at the Centre d'art contemporain - la synagogue de Delme, France. The text, published as a leaflet in French and English, was there for Robert's installation, to which the sound artist and DJ Ain Bailey associated a soundscape of female voices, in turn keeping the likes of Sturtevant, Sherrie Levine, and Louise Lawler company in the work. *Descendances du nu* traveled to different sites. Tightly bound to Robert's installation, this text was thus carried "towards its diasporic destiny." In 2017–18 it was part of *The Museum of Rhythm*, "a speculative institution that engaged rhythm as a tool for interrogating the foundations of modernity and the sensual complex of time in daily experience."[1] During the Chicago Architecture Biennial in 2019–20, the work was presented on a large nineteenth-century

1 *The Museum of Rhythm,* edited and curated by Natasha Ginwala & Daniel Muzyczuk, 2017–18.

staircase at the Chicago Cultural Center.[2] While in that city for a few days, I saw it activated by a body other than Robert's, that of a dancer to whom the moves had been assigned or delegated; its diasporic function was diffracted through other carriers as well. In 2021–22, it went to CRAC Occitanie in Sète, France, for an exhibition titled *Appui, tendu, renversé*, which was Jimmy's first large-scale institutional solo exhibition and had started at Nottingham Contemporary (UK) before traveling to Museion Bolzano in Italy.[3] *Descendances du nu* then traveled to Moderna Museet Malmö, Sweden.[4] The text too moved toward that site, before meeting the publication in which you are reading this postscript.

Why do I wish to enumerate that rather fastidious list of appearances? To me, it indicates something crucial about the work of Jimmy Robert, something that resonates with my experience of his objects, photographs, drawings, films, and performances. It stresses the inclusive crossover politics of Robert's work. Then it strongly relates to the negotiation by which each work enters

2 *...and other such stories*, Chicago Architecture Biennial 2019. Curators: Yesomi Umolu, Sepake Angiama, Paulo Tavares. The performers were Brittany Anderson, Khloe Janel, Caitlin Marz, Gina Hoch Stall, and Lily Jean Ryan.

3 *Jimmy Robert: Akimbo*, Nottingham Contemporary, 2020–21 and *Jimmy Robert: Mirror Language*, Museion Bozen-Bolzano, 2021. Curator: Bart van der Heide.

4 *Jimmy Robert: Assymetrical Grammar*, Moderna Museet Malmö, Sweden, 2023. Curator: Andreas Nilsson.

into materiality, and what "passes" from one material or medium to another. By referring to "passing," I'm referring to a survival set of body techniques used out of fear and necessity in phobic hegemonic societies. What transitions between a limping curtain, the crumpled, pleated, or rolled-up large-scale printed images of Jimmy in dancing poses, and the vulnerable bodies also subjected to collapsing, to folding, to crawling, is that which forms the work's condensed materiality. To that density, Robert attaches the dimension of theatricality—a sensible dimension, not devoid of campiness, that has to do with contact, manipulation, vulnerability. As in *Joie noire* (2019), a large printed photograph in which Robert's hands hold a book by poet and activist Gregg Bordowitz titled *General Idea: Imagevirus*,[5] folded open at the page where one finds the captioned reproduction of General Idea's *Black AIDS Painting* (1991). The "work" of the artwork is here performed twice: seen in the photographic print, and then sensed through the tiny but significant curl produced by the weight of the print exposed to gravity when pinned on a wall in the exhibition space. A body of work gives visibility to a body *at* work.

Years have passed. Josephine Baker's coffin has been inducted into the Panthéon, the hallowed tomb of white male heroes, the temple of the "great men" of France. Thousands of bodies have risen up to claim the matter

5 Gregg Bordowitz, *General Idea: Imagevirus* (London: Afterall Books), 2010.

of Black lives, acknowledging a marking out of Black bodies as the site of racialization through a process that "cannot isolate the production of racial bodies from the gendering and sexualizing of bodies."[6] Bodies at work have produced bodies *of* work.

Crumpled. Collapsed. Folded. Rolled up... Or "slightly handled," which is what this text might feel like.

6 Sara Ahmed, "Racialized Bodies" in Mary Evans and Ellie Lee (eds.), *Real Bodies* (London: Palgrave, 2002), 47. https://doi.org/10.1007/978-0-230-62974-5_4.

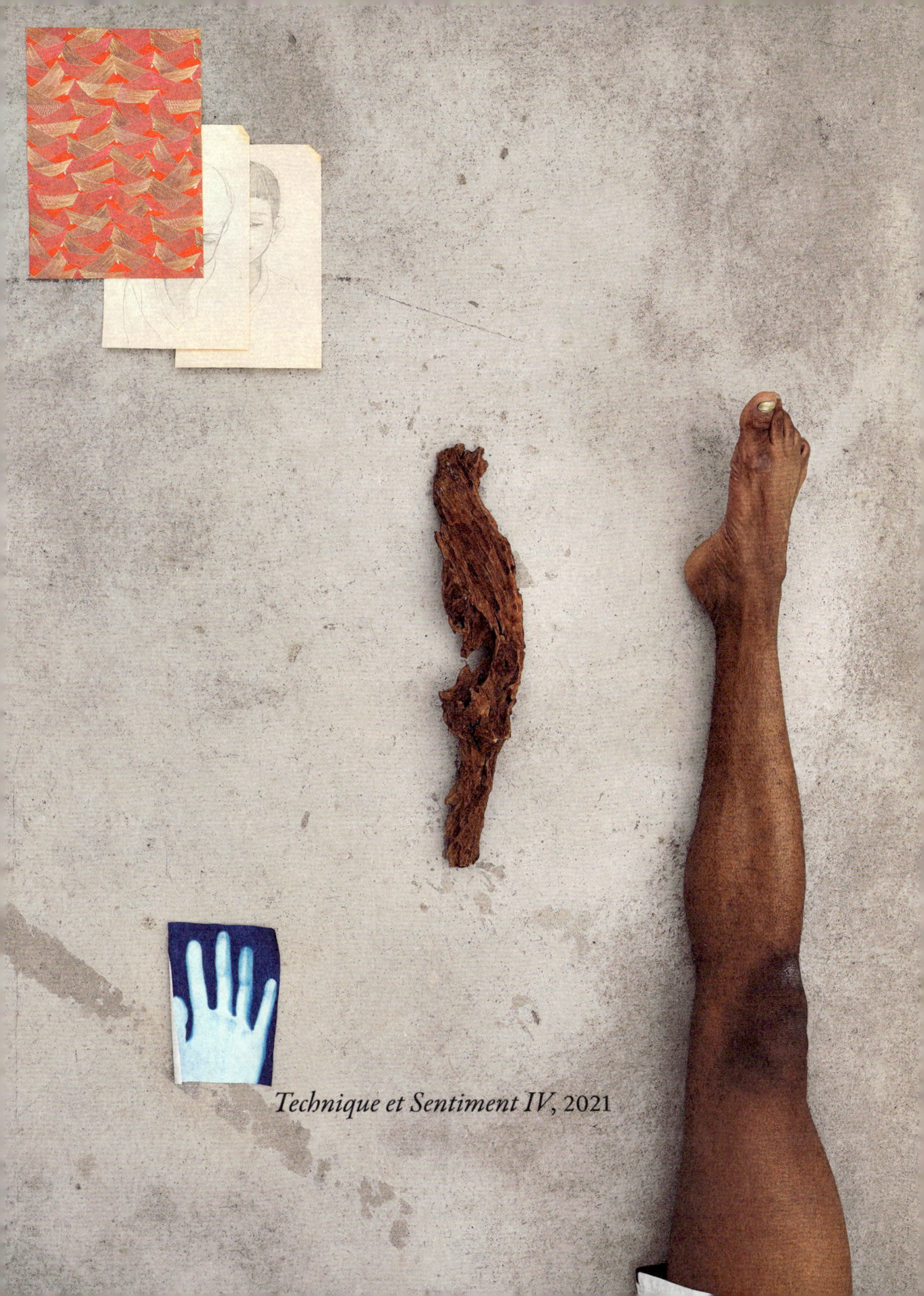

Technique et Sentiment IV, 2021

It's not lame…it's Lamé

a step too far and the image is spoilt.

a flip of the wrist at the proper angle
misconstrued as flippant resistance.

redundancy stylised,
curbed enthusiasm.

when paper falls, representation fails
read: inadequate surfaces.

Is actually Lamé really lame?

gathering momentum perhaps only
to refresh a libidinous powerlessness.

Arousing, sparkling, little trash…

vulnerability is *not* weakness
a frail body may have sharp bones

this underperforming text is a measure of how convoluted
this situation could become were you to let it unfurl.

Trompe-l'œil as trompe la mort

roll! sit! fetch!
the image won't be tamed

triumphant in the dirt
hear its lament

Nor lame, nor Lamé

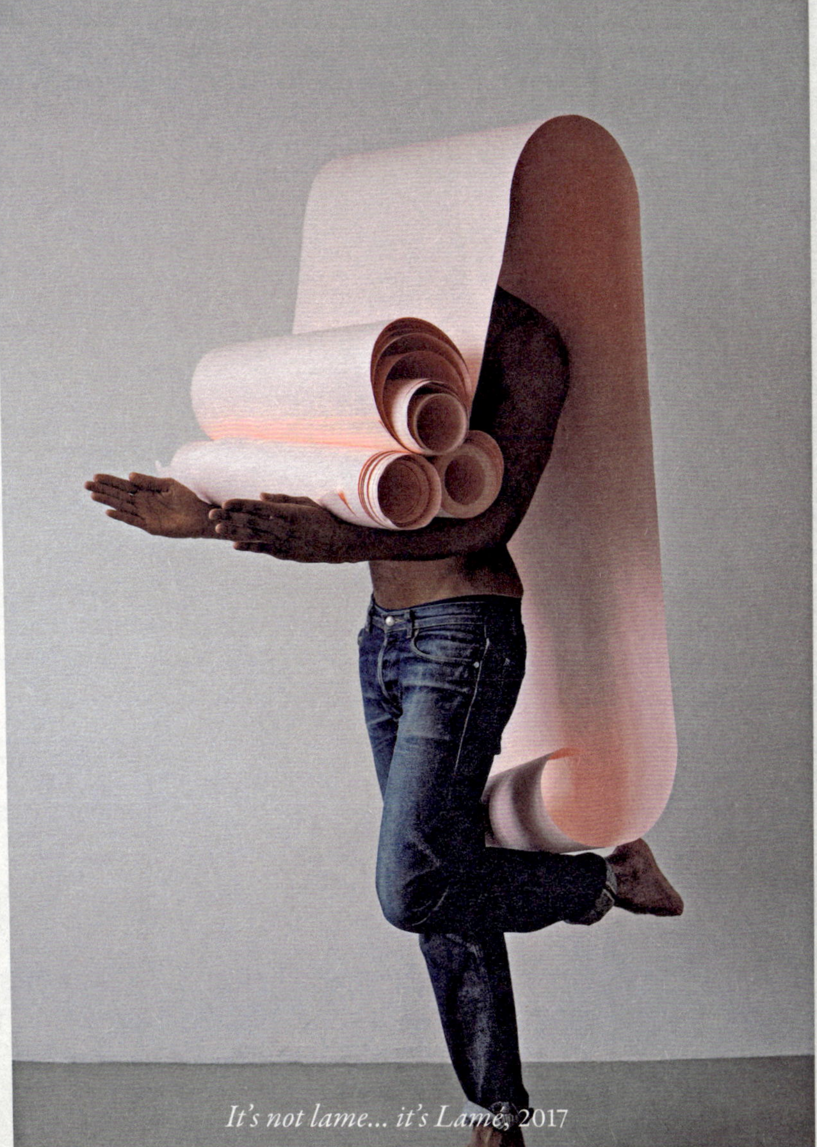

It's not lame... it's Lamé, 2017

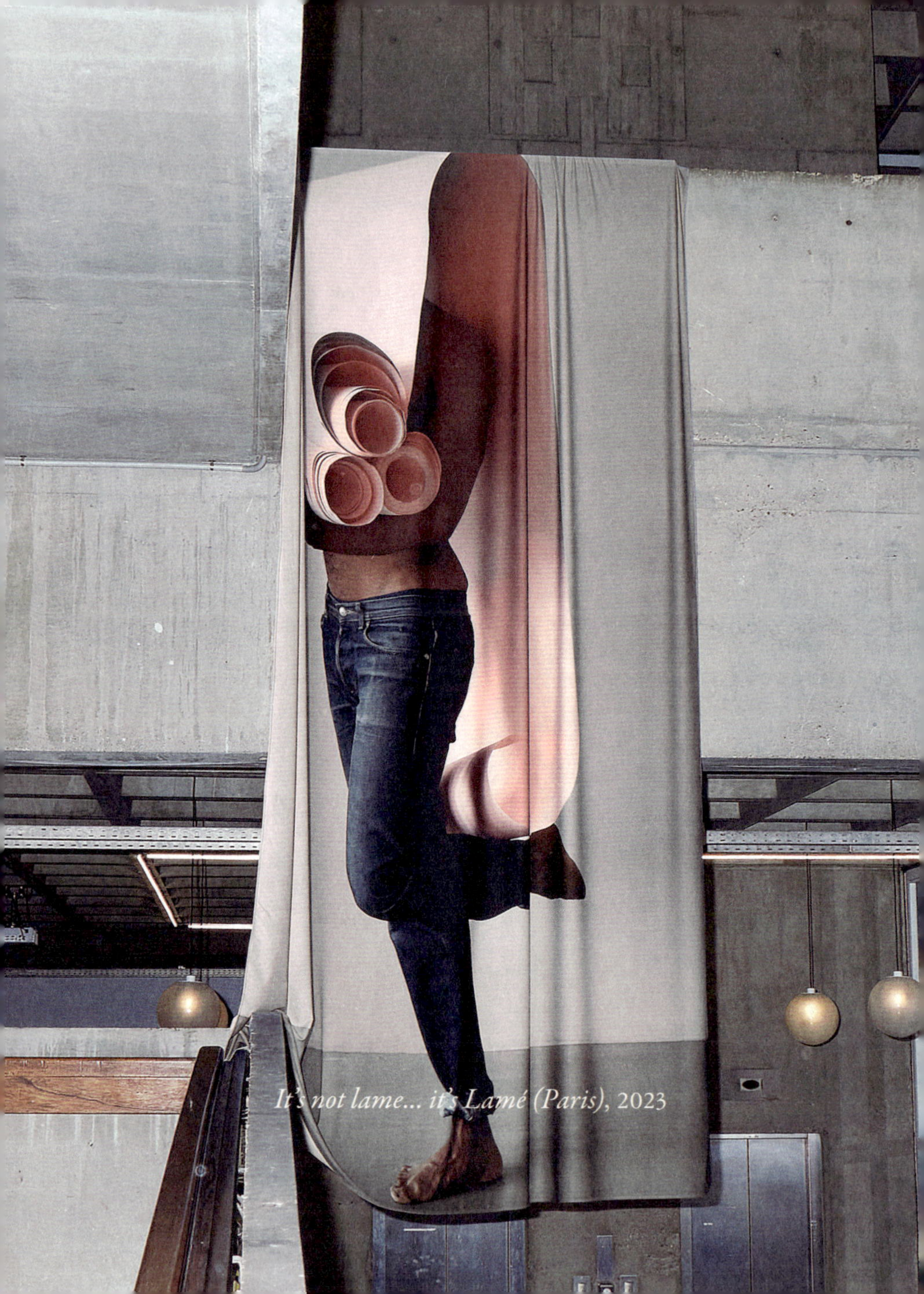

It's not lame… it's Lamé (Paris), 2023

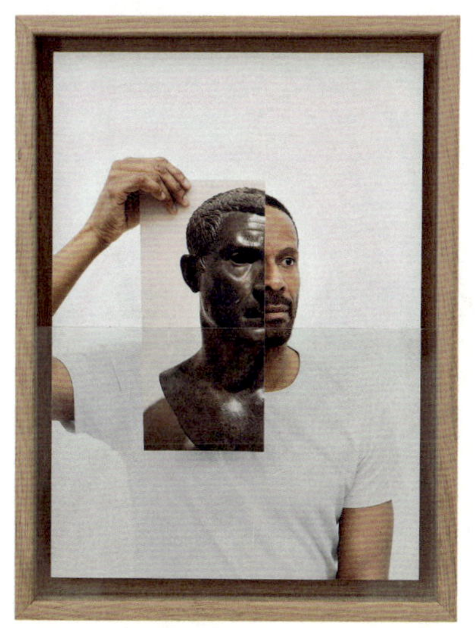

Frammenti I, 2022

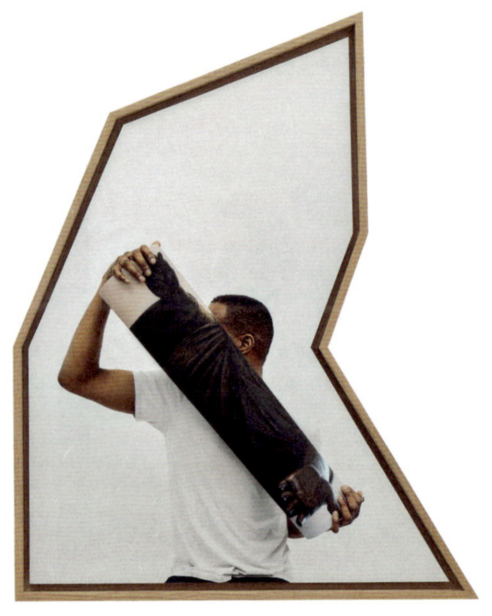

Frammenti VIII, 2022

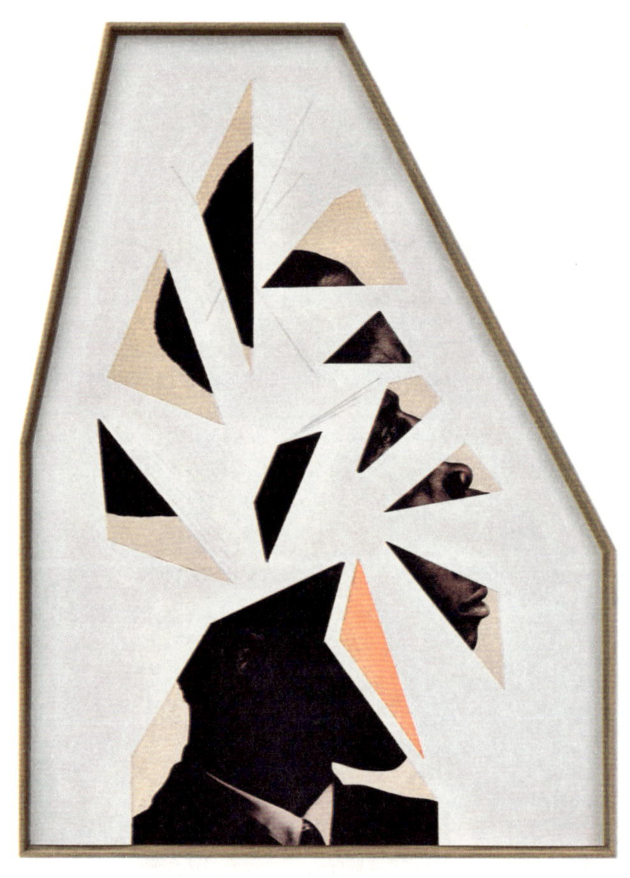

Untitled (Fragments), 2015

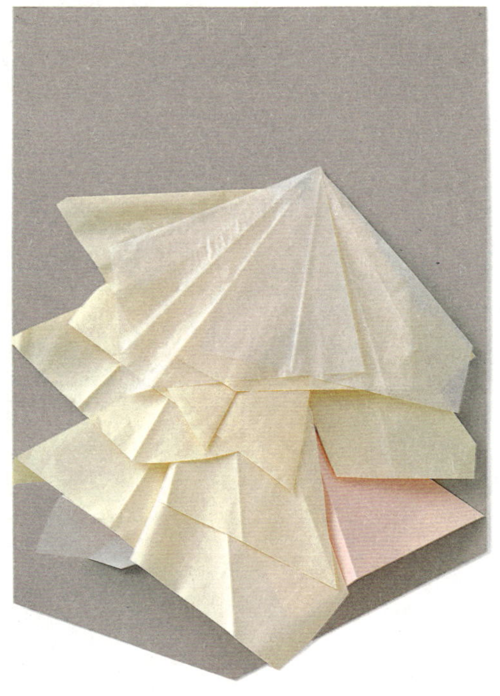

Untitled (skirt study amended), 2011

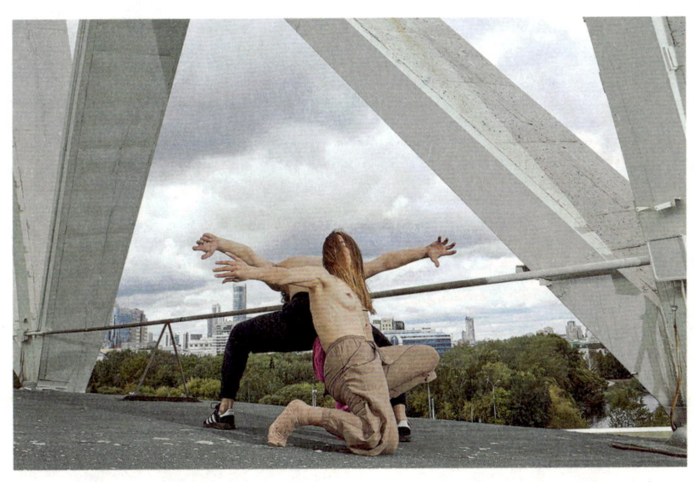

Under Amour, 2021

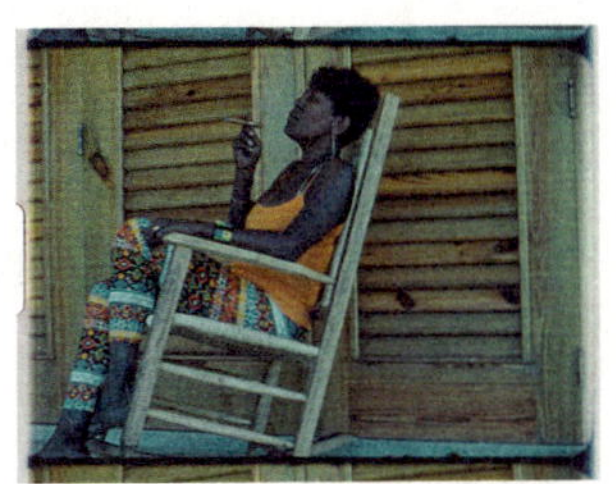

A Davidoff Cigar at Casa de Campo, 2021

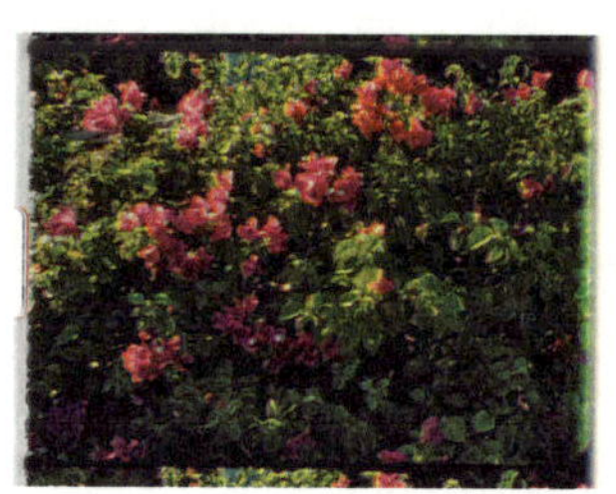

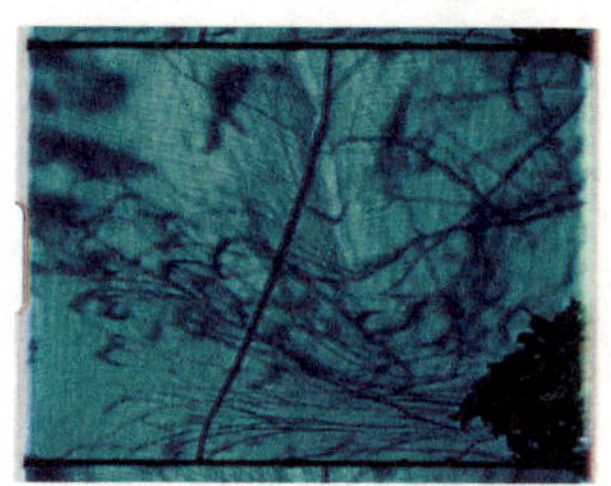

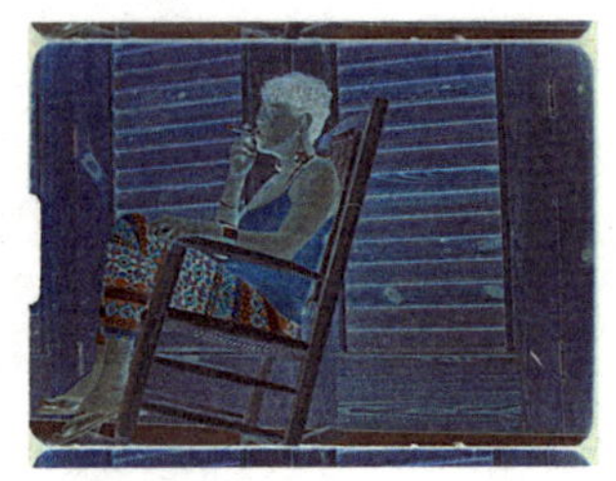

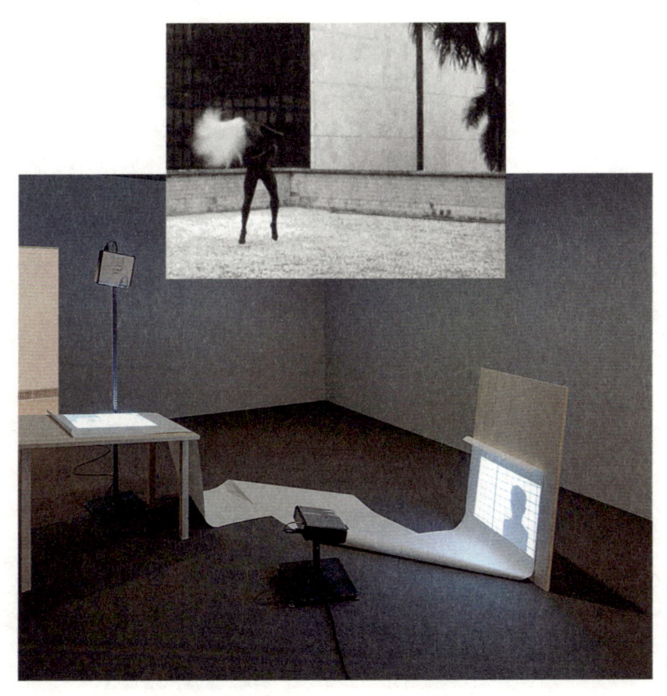

Vanishing Point, 2013

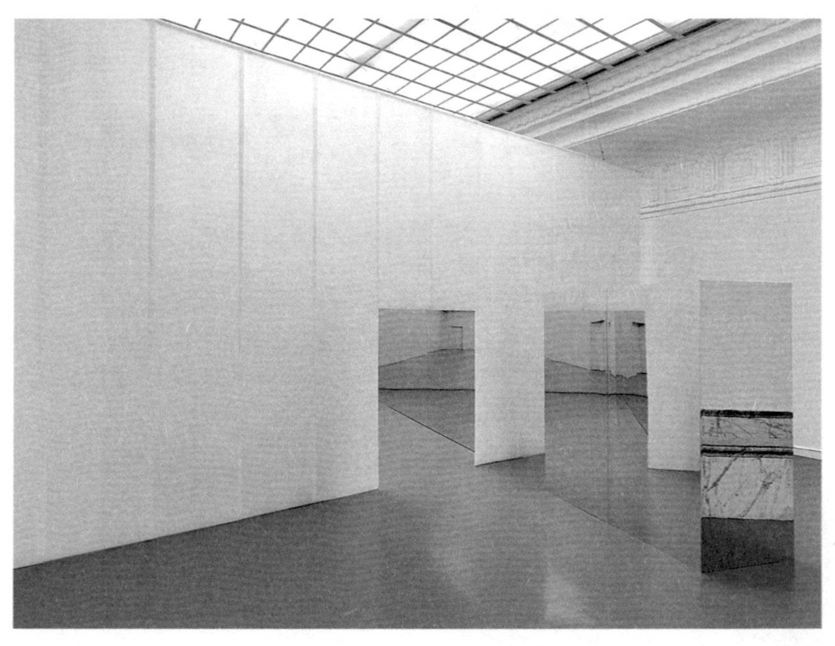

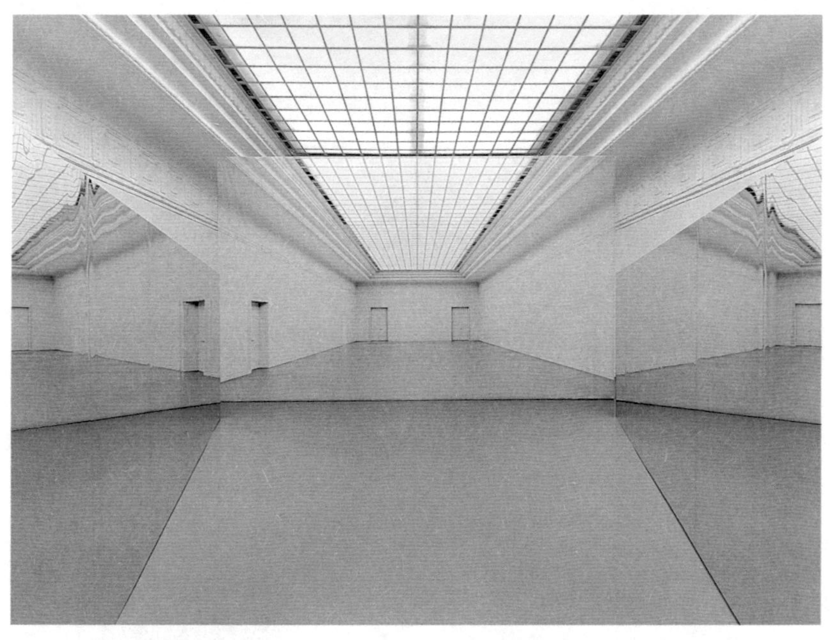

All dressed up and nowhere to go, 2023

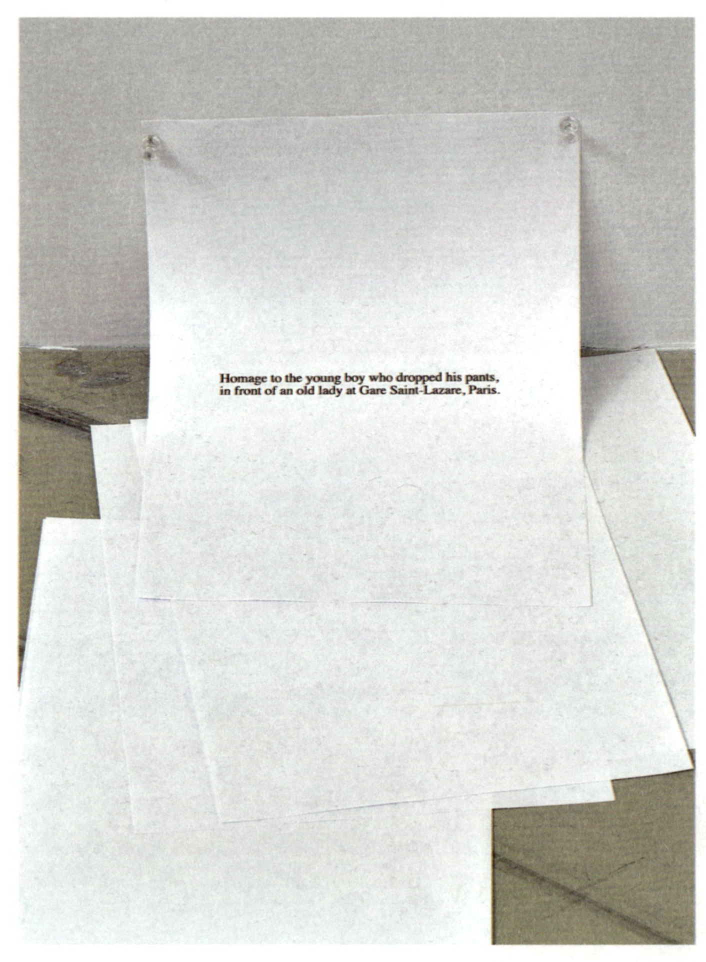

Homage to the young boy, 2007

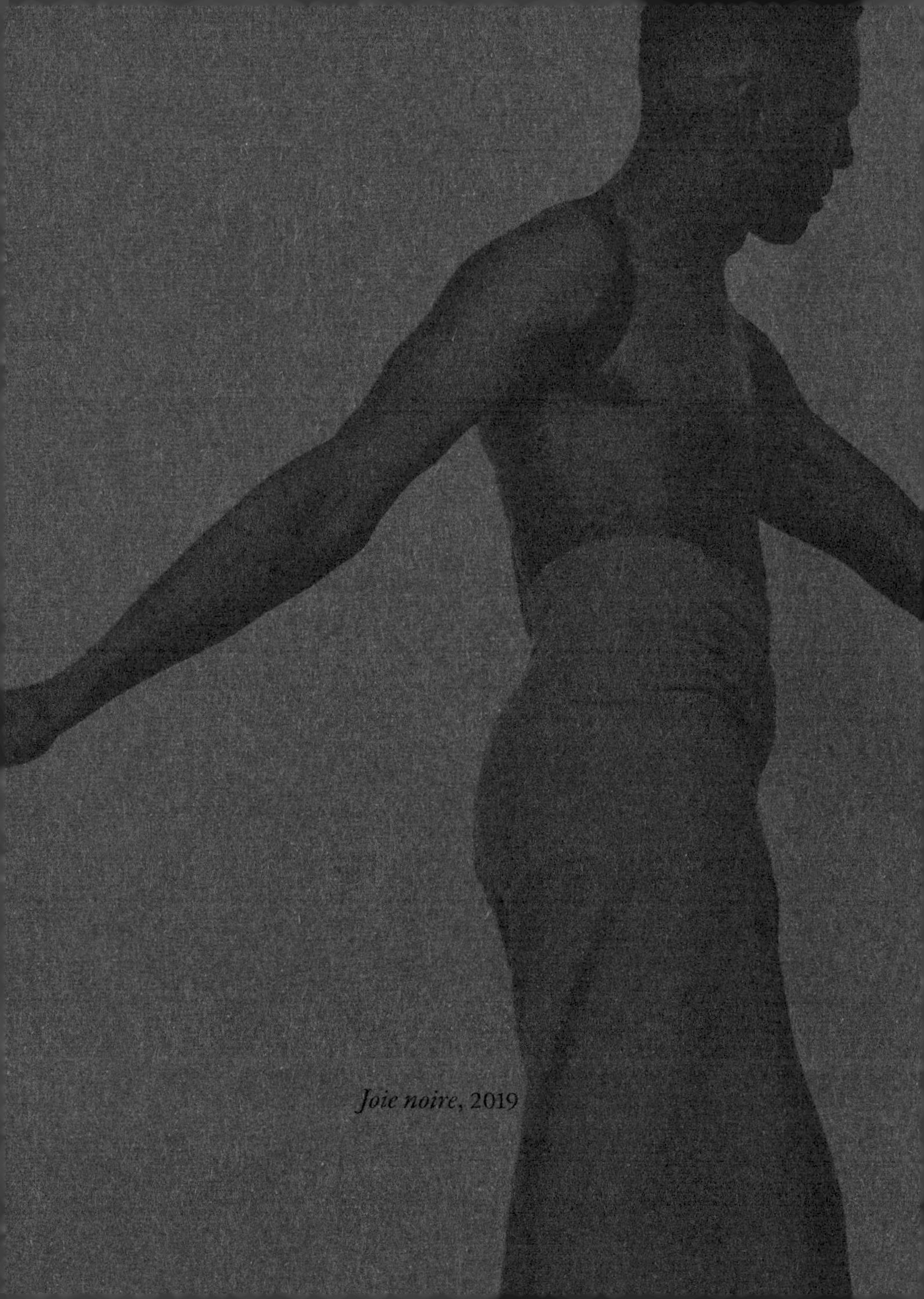

Joie noire, 2019

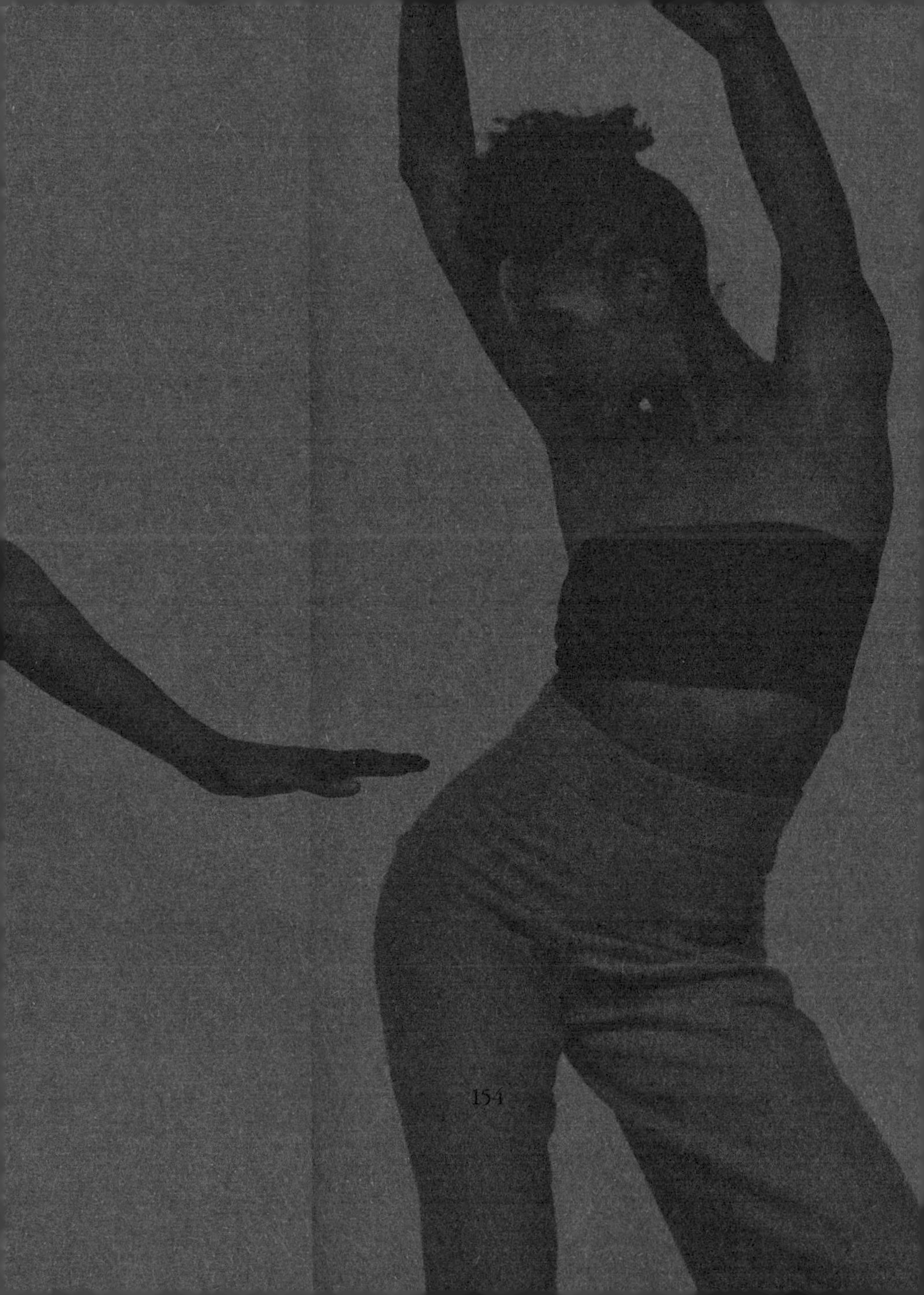

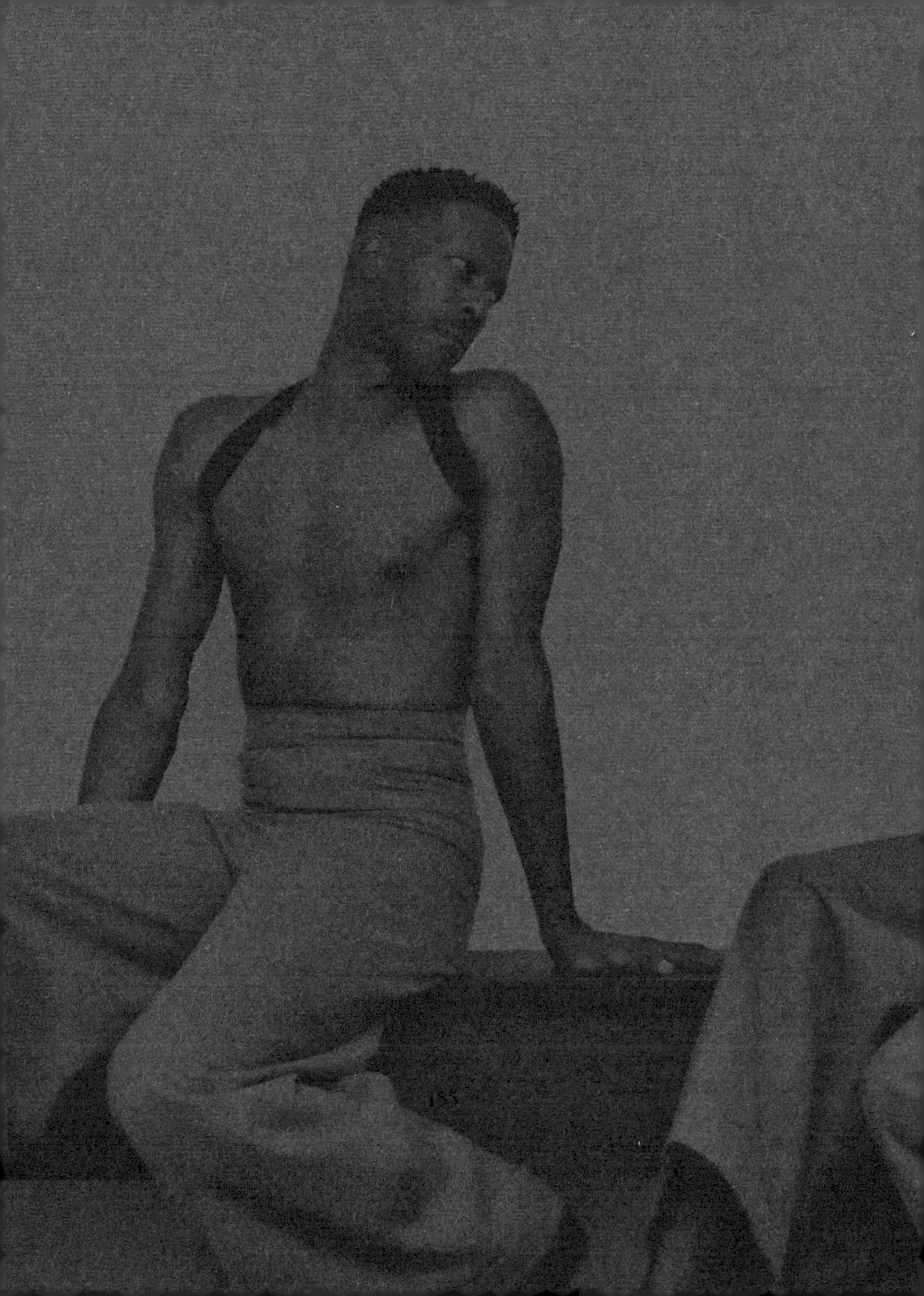

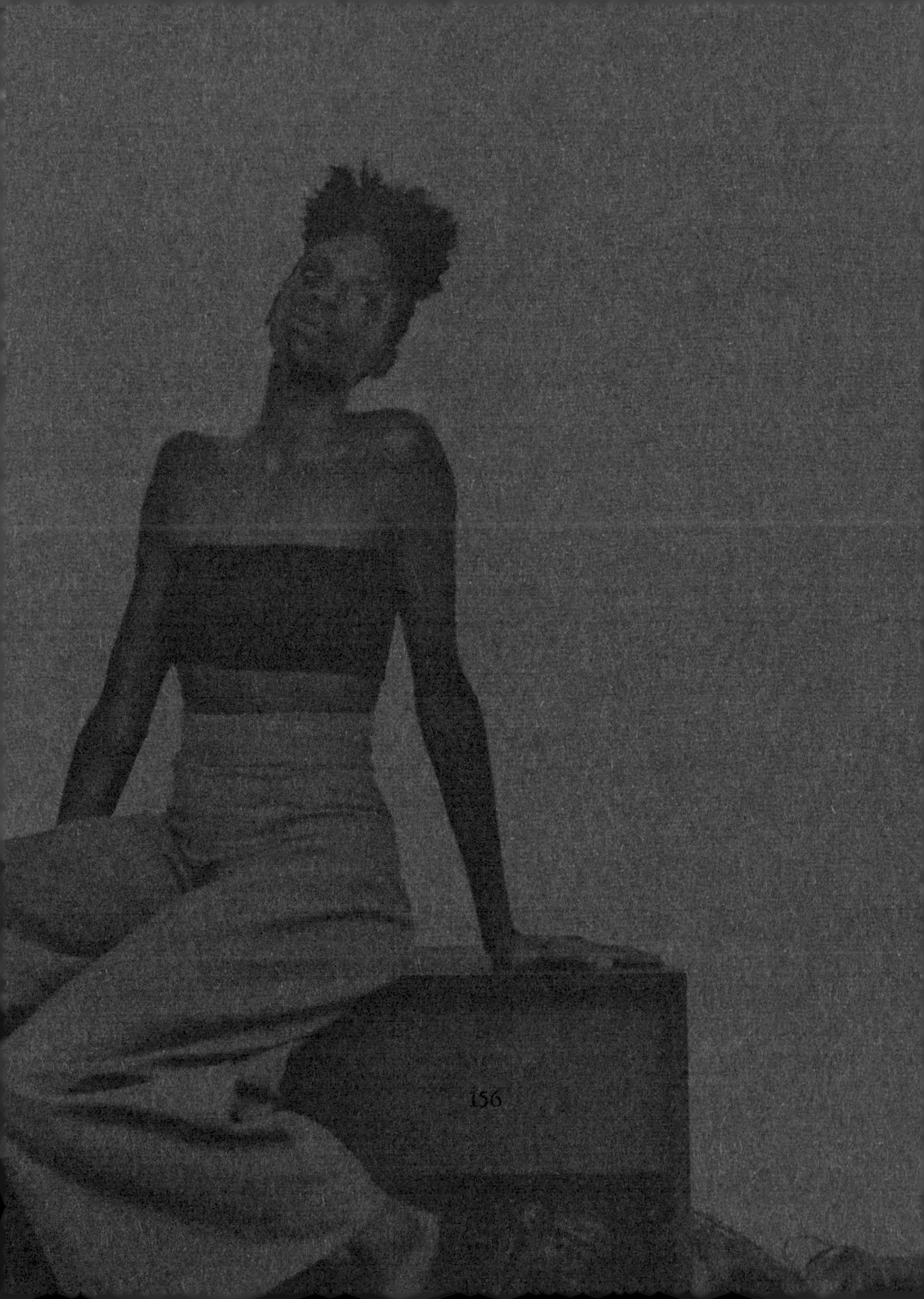

Mirror Language

Bart van der Heide

In the winter of 1963, the influential conceptual artist Stanley Brouwn (Surinam, 1935–Amsterdam, 2017) placed sheets of white drawing paper (24.5 × 32 cm) on the pavements of Amsterdam's city center. After twenty-four hours, Brouwn returned to the site and collected the sheets that now registered the traces of numerous pedestrians. His aim to capture intangible elements in our daily lives, such as time and memory, led the artist to portray fleeting moments in a day in the form of the traces we leave behind. The resulting work, entitled *View of a City in 24 Hours* (1963), is a captivating document of anonymous people going, as he described it, "from a to b."

In the past, the blank page has been repeatedly identified by artists and writers as the main source of their anxiety and imagined inadequacy. When charged with the expectations of communication, the empty page means everything and nothing at the same time. Words and letters can partly overcome the anxiety when they trace the author's intention, like footsteps in the snow.

Words are a way for the reader to move on and become one with a larger geography of thought and experience.

However, as *View of a City in 24 Hours* (1963) affirms, words (like footsteps) can never offer a comprehensive picture of this geography when it comes to identification and time. This led French structuralist writers of the late 1960s, such as the journalist/thinker Maurice Blanchot, to focus more on the empty spaces between the words instead of on the words themselves. From this perspective, any form of comprehension should be suspended at all cost, whether it concerns Aristotelian unity or Hegelian totality. Meaningful literature had to be built out of fragments, vignettes, segments, documents, or chapters that might be read in isolation and/or as part of the greater whole. The fleeting moments in between the fragments, when the dots had to be connected, were prioritized and became the main force behind meaning, evoking active integration with the "here and now" of the reading experience.

It comes as no surprise that both Brouwn and Blanchot have had a fundamental impact on Jimmy Robert's artistic practice. *Mirror Language* features the first European survey and the Italian debut of this Guadeloupe-born French artist (b. 1975), highlighting an artistic practice that is firmly placed on the disciplinary intersection between literature, poetry, and visual art. His artworks enable dialogue between imagery and text, text and movement, performance and objecthood that can be experienced in isolation as well as part of a larger syntax. The exhibition brings together writing, collage, photography, sculpture, and performance produced by Robert over the last twenty years. What comes across is that the individual artworks depict a momentary transition in which an existing experience or narrative is captured and passed on: "from a to b."

For instance, the life of an artwork can begin with a found portrait—sourced from art history books, historical photographs, family albums, or periodicals—to which the artist adds a piece of pleated paper or tape that shifts the images into the third dimension. Robert speaks about these source images as pictures of people who are "performing" or are aware of being seen. Treating them as live subjects, Robert obstructs their sensory faculties; eyes, nose, and mouth are often covered or torn away, rendering the subject blind or mute. This coins an evolutionary process through which the artist continues to reproduce and re-appropriate these same images on consecutive occasions, creating a trace of artifice and added layers. A collage is scanned, enhanced, and reprinted, whereby it may even continue to transform into an autonomous sculpture, a prop in a performance, or into abstract gestures embodied by the artist himself.

At the heart of this fragmented expansion lies the question of authorship itself. Stanley Brouwn was known for eradicating the artist-subject all together, making him Conceptual Art's biggest enigma. Blanchot was more interested in what the author didn't mention and less in the words written on the page. Robert distinctively highlights the vulnerability of the artist-subject by raising the question of to what extent a muted voice can leave an imprint. Not only are the materials he uses experienced as humble and disposable—paper, adhesive tape, and plywood—the works on show in *Mirror Language* are, in theory, unfinished. They are placeholders of broader reflections on legacy, a value that continues to be racialized and gendered today. This is why one single work can never capture its complete meaning in isolation, because when a voice is muted, other forms of transmission come into play that might be transient in nature but still guarantee a trace. Hence, an artwork by Robert initiates a temporary moment in which knowledge is embodied and passed on through learning, teaching, translation, and mirroring.

Throughout the exhibition, the works are organized and selected around large sheets of paper that split up the open layout of the exhibition space with makeshift walls. The artworks are installed on top of and around the sheets, like the footprints on the paper Stanley Brouwn left on that Amsterdam pavement. Some works are even printed directly onto the paper, an echo of their own originality. Texts that were originally written in English or French are translated for a German- and Italian-speaking audience and added to the original texts as an appendix. One might say that, with this installation, the artist enables yet another layer of reproduction and embodiment to propose a new temporal footprint.

Like many others in the art world, Jimmy Robert never met Stanley Brouwn in person. A letter he sent to the artist in 2013 remained unanswered. Nevertheless, this same letter—ending with the words "May this text be an indication of the space between you and me"—became the starting point for a set of works by Robert under the title *Many Shades of Brouwn*, which can be seen as an elicited response. *Mirror Language* features the installation *Untitled (Brouwn)*, which consists of a wooden table adapted to a 140 × 100 cm scan of the handwritten letter. Part of the letter is obscured by fragments of an original artwork.

Mirror Language also features references to historic performance artists such as Yvonne Rainer (San Francisco, 1934), Bas Jan Ader (Winschoten, 1942–Atlantic Ocean, 1975), and Bruce Nauman (Fort Wayne, 1941). Over the last few years, their legacy has been at the center of critical discourse, within both art and dance worlds. As many performances in the early 1960s were exclusively reliant on the body of the artist, discussions arise on how these works will be experienced in the future. Of course, for Bas Jan Ader, loss was at the heart of his practice already. The fact that he himself disappeared prematurely on the open sea, never to return, has contributed to the wide-ranging imagery of his work. Bruce Nauman, on the other hand, found a solution by writing an instruction manual (produced between 1969 and 1975). These instructions stem from the artist's engagement with traditional sculptural processes of casting and mold-making, and focus the reader's attention on their own corporeality.

With *Cadavre Exquis* (2010), Jimmy Robert transformed Nauman's instructions by applying an interactive game with same name. In the game *cadavre exquis*, originally invented by the Surrealists, players write in turn on a sheet of paper, fold it to conceal part of the writing, and then pass it to the next player for a further contribution. The end result is a fragmented poem that invites future readers to connect the dots of something intentionally incoherent. Here, following Blanchot's writing, the empty spaces between the sentences have become so large that "a to b" seems to be a world within itself.

Consequently, Jimmy Robert folded Nauman's pragmatic instructions in such a way that part of them are obscured and others stand out, creating a poem in the style of Stéphane Mallarmé in which large sections are visually erased. Robert made the instructions his own, while also allowing room for further interpretation: in Jimmy Robert's work, legacy is not defined by language or singular messages, but is always transformative and defined by practice.

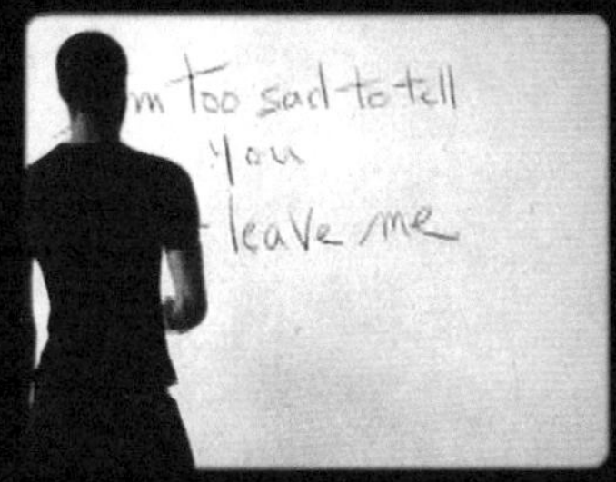

L'éducation sentimentale, 2005

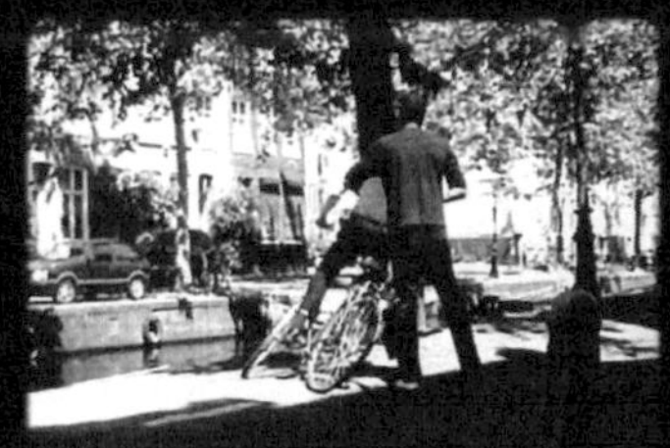

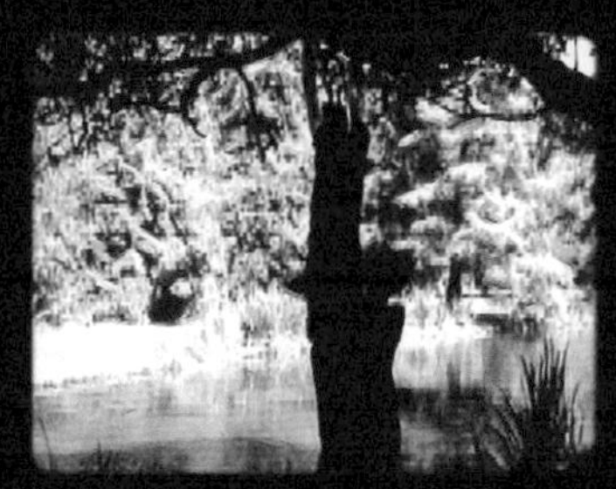

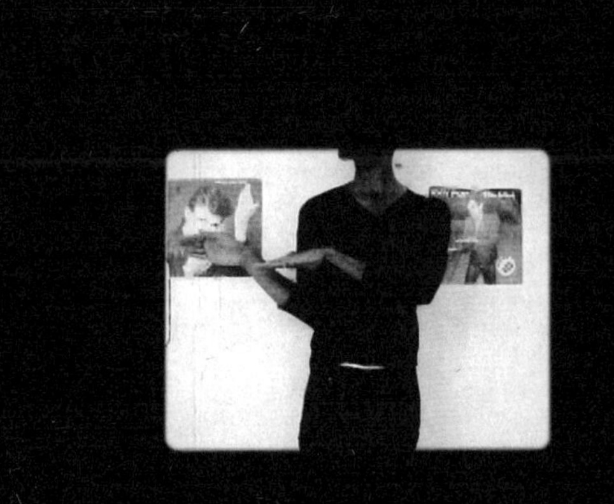

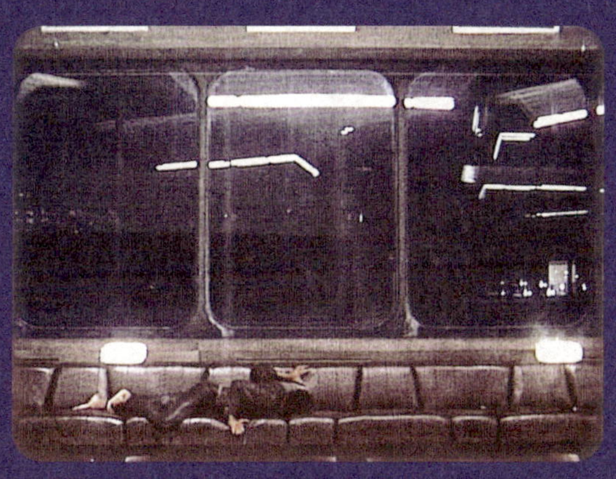

Brown Leatherette, 2002

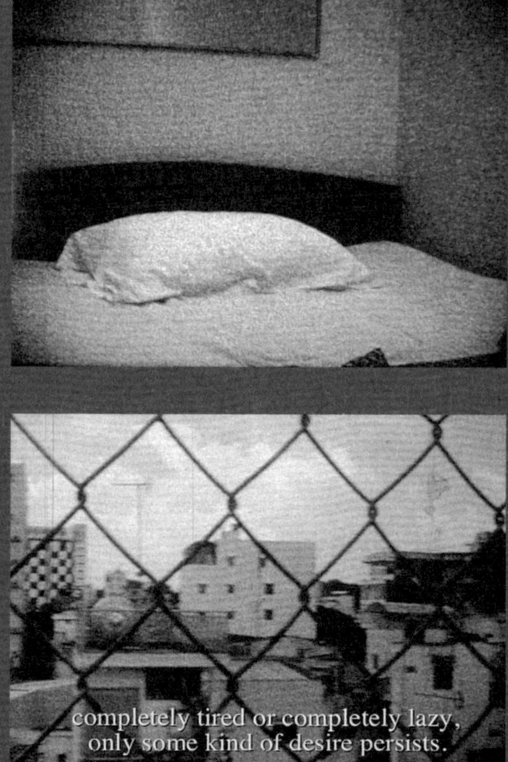

French film, 2000

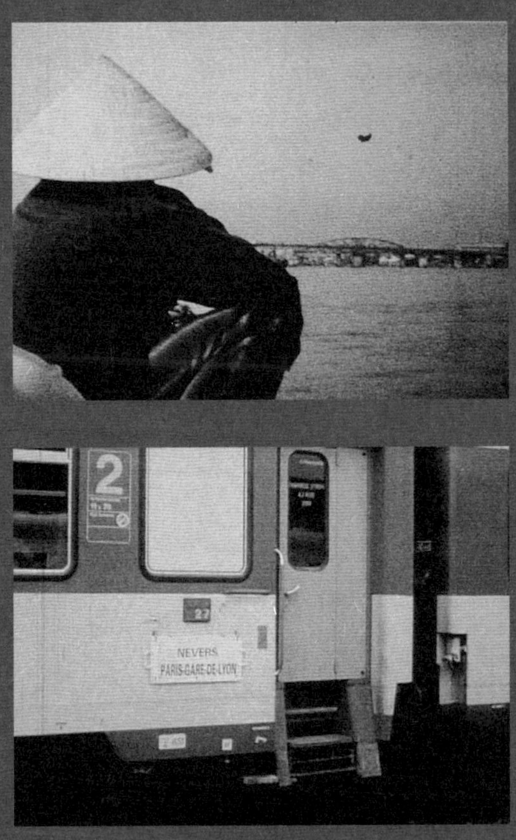
2
27
NEVERS
PARIS-GARE-DE-LYON

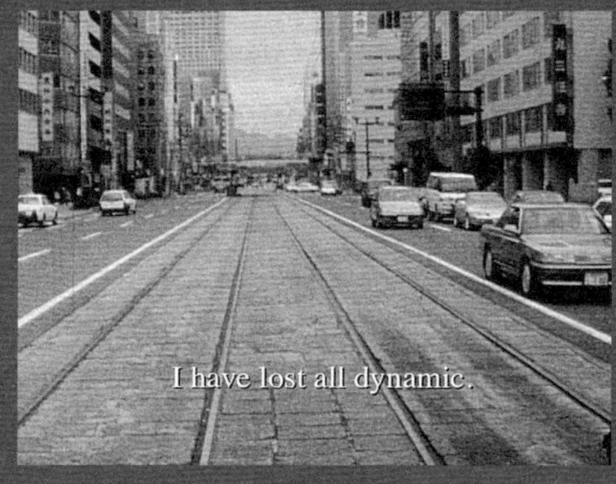
I have lost all dynamic.

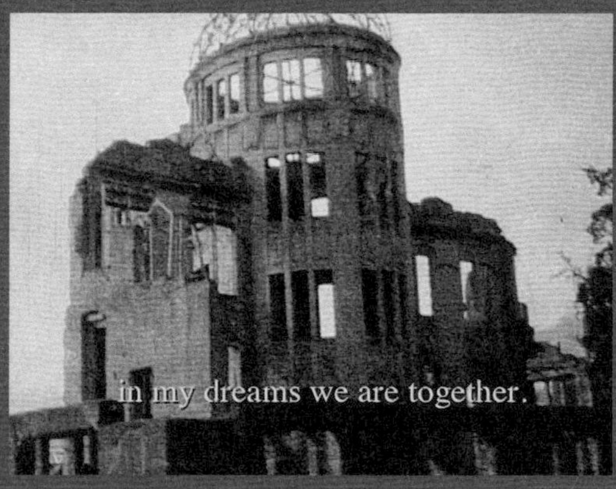
in my dreams we are together.

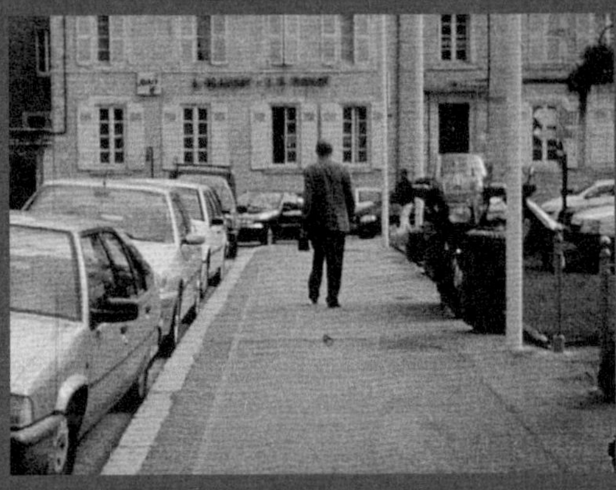

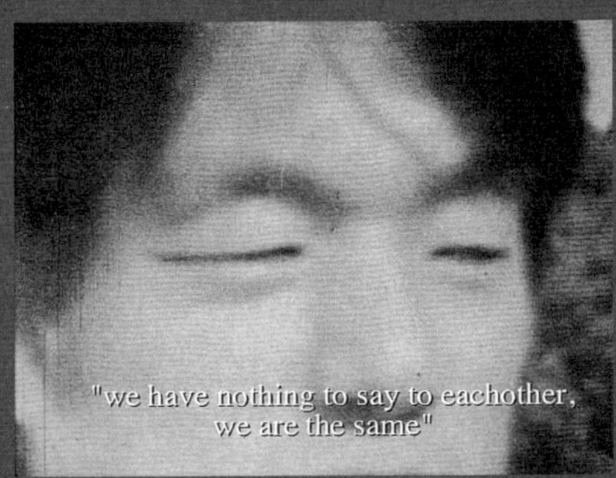
"we have nothing to say to eachother,
we are the same"

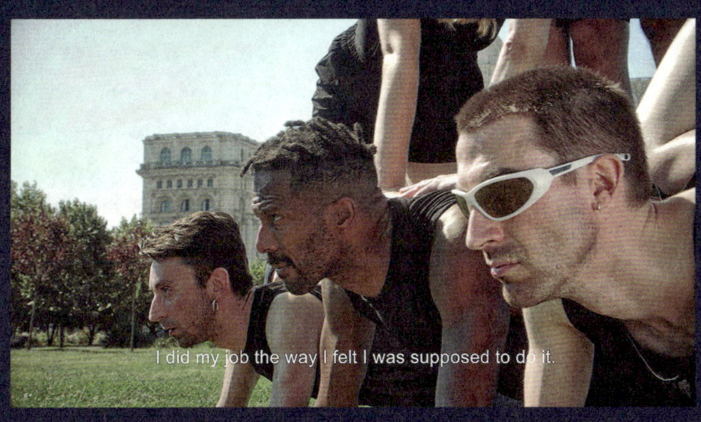

Cruising, 2019

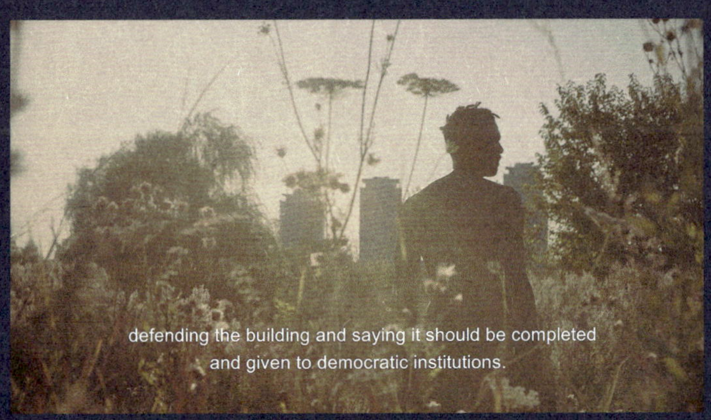
defending the building and saying it should be completed
and given to democratic institutions.

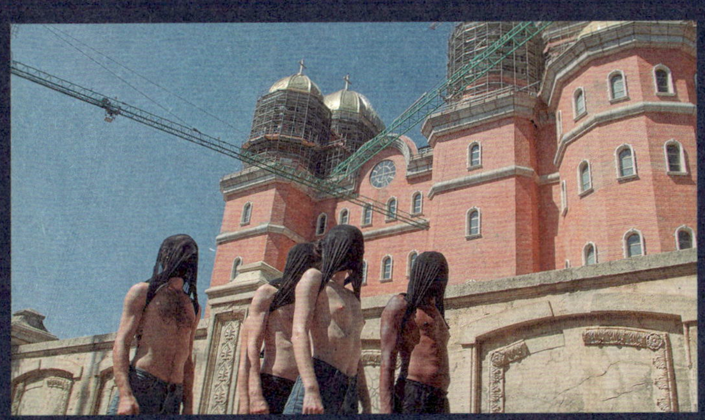

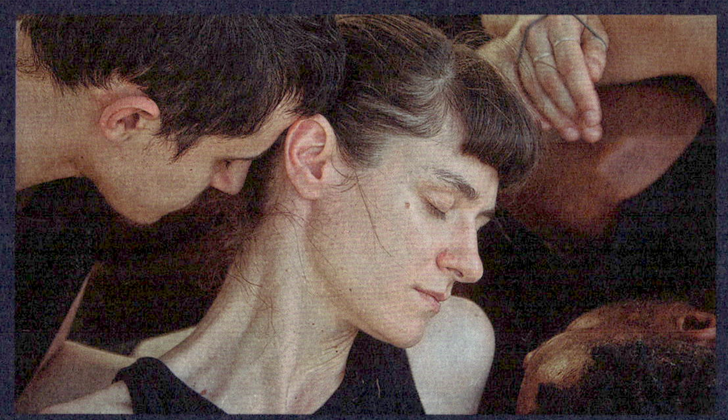

F+Q
A Joint Reflection on Jimmy Robert's Practice

Çağla İlk and Misal Adnan Yıldız

Çağla İlk and Misal Adnan Yıldız go on a blind experimental writing date. Without knowing what the other is writing and not working on the same document, they each reflect on Jimmy Robert's oeuvre and investigate his impact on their understanding of performance and art. Only later, talking and reflecting for long hours across the distance between Venice and Baden-Baden, will they bring their bits of writing together for the deadline of this publication.

F
Passage to performativity through the poetical

Çağla İlk

By writing a text in which we acknowledge the plurality of collaborations of the artists we work with, we make ourselves aware of how these interactions shape our identity.

Yvonne Rainer and Jimmy Robert's passage to performativity

In the early 2000s, Jimmy Robert and the artist, film curator, and writer Ian White (1971–2013) were preparing *6 things we couldn't do, but can do now* for Tate Britain when they contacted Yvonne Rainer and her collaborator Pat Catterson in order to learn the dance *Trio A* (1965), Rainer's pioneering choreographic work. *Trio A* is based on continuous fully choreographed movements, transitioning smoothly from one gesture to another, incorporating elements from ballet as well as the everyday. It was intended to be accessible to dancers and nondancers of all backgrounds; some have termed this approach "democratic choreography."

In my interview with Catterson in January 2023 at the Kunsthalle Baden-Baden, before the premiere of Rainer's last piece, *HELLZAPOPPIN': What about the bees?* she said that Rainer was very particular about who she allowed to learn *Trio A*. White and Robert, whom they called "The Tall Boys / Tate Boys," got permission easily. Catterson provided them with the manuals and suggested they engage in movement-based exercises like tai chi prior to the rehearsals to familiarize their bodies with the discipline. She observed their dedication during lengthy rehearsals and their ability to suffer incredible pain without complaint. She was impressed by their ambition even though they were "non-dancers." Dressed in jeans and T-shirts, Robert and White staged *Trio A* as part of *6 things we couldn't do, but can do now* at Tate Britain in 2004.

This was a pivotal moment in Robert's artistic practice: it was through *6 things...* that he adopted the performative approach of a conceptual dancer.

Robert draws inspiration from performance and poetry and extends his inspiration to photography, which he sensually links to key figures such as Rainer.

The written as poetry and connection to future and past

Robert's work, as poetic as it is in itself, often also has poetry in it. As exemplified in *Floor Work*, a poem written

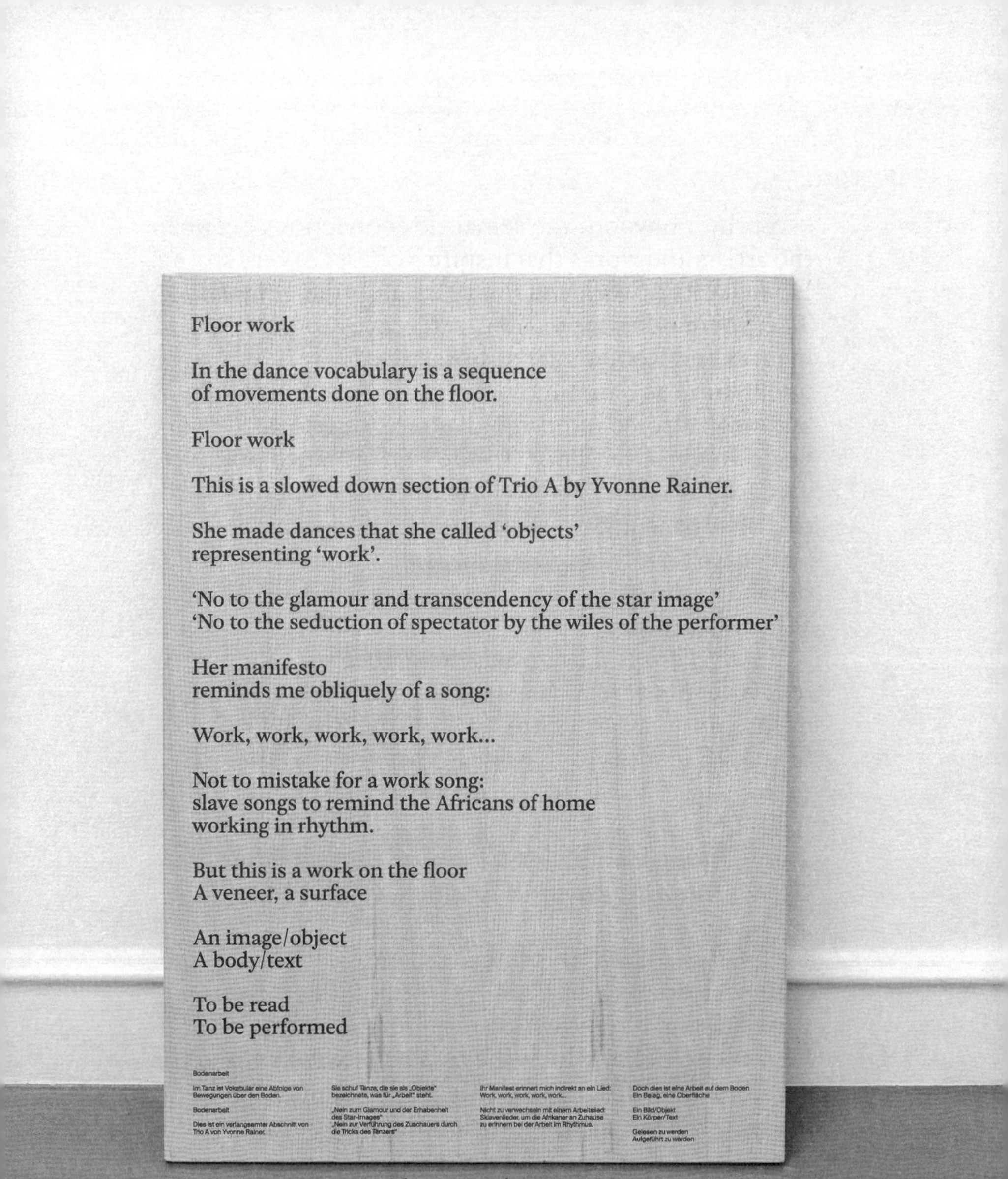

Floor work

In the dance vocabulary is a sequence
of movements done on the floor.

Floor work

This is a slowed down section of Trio A by Yvonne Rainer.

She made dances that she called ‘objects’
representing ‘work’.

‘No to the glamour and transcendency of the star image’
‘No to the seduction of spectator by the wiles of the performer’

Her manifesto
reminds me obliquely of a song:

Work, work, work, work, work...

Not to mistake for a work song:
slave songs to remind the Africans of home
working in rhythm.

But this is a work on the floor
A veneer, a surface

An image/object
A body/text

To be read
To be performed

Bodenarbeit

Im Tanz ist Vokabular eine Abfolge von
Bewegungen über den Boden.

Bodenarbeit

Dies ist ein verlangsamter Abschnitt von
Trio A von Yvonne Rainer.

Sie schuf Tänze, die sie als „Objekte"
bezeichnete, was für „Arbeit" steht.

„Nein zum Glamour und der Erhabenheit
des Star-Images"
„Nein zur Verführung des Zuschauers durch
die Tricks des Tänzers"

Ihr Manifest erinnert mich indirekt an ein Lied:
Work, work, work, work, work...

Nicht zu verwechseln mit einem Arbeitslied:
Sklavenlieder, um die Afrikaner an Zuhause
zu erinnern bei der Arbeit im Rhythmus.

Doch dies ist eine Arbeit auf dem Boden
Ein Belag, eine Oberfläche

Ein Bild/Objekt
Ein Körper/Text

Gelesen zu werden
Aufgeführt zu werden

Floor Work, 2020

as a print on wood, the semantic connections between the artists and works that inspire Robert are very strong. He made this work sixteen years after dancing *Trio A*. The poem contains various references to past performances and Robert's artistic practice. *Floor Work* can be understood as dance movements executed on the floor, but it can also be interpreted as referring to an artwork positioned on the floor. In the performance of dance, while aging affects the body, the evolution of the body's response to dance presents another dimension.

For Robert, an important aspect of Rainer's *Trio A* is the abduction of the gaze: the dancers never look directly at the audience.

Floor Work is a linguistic twist that simultaneously reflects the performance and the sociohistorical connotations of music. It opens up a perspective on vulnerability and identity.

Under Amour: *Imitation and empowerment according to the class and body of beings*

Under Amour (2021) was primarily conceived as a site-specific performance in a still fully operating traditional Russian state circus in Yekaterinburg as part of the 6th Ural Biennale, of which the two of us were among the curators. It addressed the fragility of the human body, often concealed by strength, a skill paramount to circus performers and acrobats. The artists sought to distinguish between the notions of armor and love, which turn out to be very close, since they both grapple with the issue of human vulnerability. In his afterword to the English edition of Jacques Rancière's *The Politics of Aesthetics* in 2004, Slavoj Žižek asked: "So when, three decades ago, Kung Fu films were popular (Bruce Lee, etc.), was it not obvious that we were dealing with a genuine working-class ideology of youngsters whose only means of success was the disciplinary training of their only possession, their bodies?"[1] Similarly, Vijay Prashad, in his 2001 book on African-Asian relations, had noted that martial arts culture has historically created political solidarity and cross-racial identification among oppressed peoples worldwide.[2]

Robert's project centered on depictions of trained individuals executing various kung-fu poses, often reminiscent of animals in circus arenas. This inevitably evoked parallels to the human exhibitions prevalent around the turn of the twentieth century, where individuals of Asian and African descent were inhumanely showcased. *Under Amour* seemed to pose questions such as: How are martial arts viewed today? Is this type of knowledge still

1 Slavoj Žižek, "Afterword: The Lesson of Rancière," in Jacques Rancière, *The Politics of Aesthetics*, trans. Gabriel Rockhill (London: Continuum, 2004), 78.

2 See Vijay Prashad, *Everybody was Kung Fu Fighting: Afro-Asian Connections and the Myth of Cultural Purity*, (Boston, MA: Beacon Press 2001).

empowering? Can it still protect us? What is our relationship with the East through this embodied cultural knowledge? What do we learn from animals, and have we become any wiser?

In the context of the Ural Biennale, we encountered a passage from performativity to installation, each representing a different phase of an ongoing work. Performative moments gave way to poetic photographs of frozen gestures dispersed throughout the circus venue—from the dressing rooms to the foyer to the seats for the audience—inviting contemplation and envisioning around the performance.

The gaze on the self and the poetics of the frozen

We could say that Robert uses the medium of photography like a writer's pen. He freezes moments in a fragile way, describing them with detailed precision.

Our conversations on the gaze and its orientation were primarily rooted in these descriptive moments. At Kunsthalle Baden-Baden, which I codirect with Misal Adnan Yıldız, our curatorial proposal for all exhibitions is focused on developing moments and transitional forms that continually evolve throughout their observation. And what happens when the body disappears? We invite our audiences to create the performance themselves and submerge into the experience.

For me, Robert's 2022 solo exhibition in Baden-Baden, a traditional spa town where strolling has always been the predominant human movement, stands out as one of his most significant site-specific works, precisely addressing this notion. Given that the act of self-expression through promenading is ingrained in the city's inhabitants, the artist's approach to the urban environment revolved around the idea of observation and visibility.

In this context, the title of the exhibition, *All dressed up and nowhere to go*, raised questions of belonging, the position one assumes through clothing and movement, through one's own observations and the gaze of others.

The labyrinthine mirror-based architecture that Robert installed created both a stage and a backstage, setting the scene for introspection in the exhibition space of a state institution. Visitors were invited to contemplate their own visibility and presence while reflecting on the historical context of white walls and the long-standing invisibility of BIPOC bodies in public spaces and art institutions.

In various displayed photographs, Robert occupied the "stage," in costume and guided by a small but significant number of elements: the marble balustrade became a pedestal, for example, similar to those bearing the sculptures in front of the Kunsthalle entrance; it merged with the walls, doors, and staircase. Approaching such restrictive architecture, which is not intended for people's tactile encounters, these images bolstered the exhibition title and its corresponding poses. As frozen moments of performance, they resembled paintings that seemed to attempt to objectify or elevate the artist to the status of sculpture, to place himself in a frame that does not allow this.

Through the work and its architectural references, Jimmy Robert referred metaphorically to the limiting patterns of our thought and viewing habits. The eyes that did not meet the audience in *Trio A* voluntarily disconnected from the audience in *All dressed up and nowhere to go*. Perhaps the eyes were bleached; they resembled a zombie's.

Robert's artworks are thus distinguished by non-linear dramaturgy and networks of spatial connections. His approach is unique. Materially, formally, and in terms of format, he seamlessly combines the poetic and the political. This is what has secured my dedication to his body of work, in the past and into the future.

Q
Queer controversy

Misal Adnan Yıldız

Do you know what "falsified memory" means?

Prince's 1984 song "When Doves Cry" is about to celebrate its fortieth birthday.[3] After watching the video again, I found that an image from my childhood had gained flesh and bone. I remember standing in front of a TV; it was probably a cold winter evening, I wore a stripey pullover, and what I saw on that TV fascinated me. I am not sure if what I recall now can be precisely true. I am not sure whether it was Prince or Zeki Müren or mathematics. Whether I was five years old or older... At what age—maybe with a delay in Anatolia—Prince and the Revolution shook the ground I stood on, my world, our house, and the rest of the planet. Much later, when all the teens around me couldn't choose between Michael Jackson and Madonna, I was stuck between Freddie Mercury, George Michael, and Prince. For clear reason. A photo exists of me dancing in front of the TV, facing

3 Prince the singer was often referred to as The Artist Formerly Known as Prince (or TAFKAP) or simply The Artist but he was also known to fans as the "Love Symbol."

my audience of aunts and my parents. It was probably taken by my father, the most anxious person in the room.

In most of my professional engagements within the arts there has been some space for bringing in conversations, concepts, and terms from psychology and my background in social science. Falsified memory is a situation in which a person's recollection of an event or information is incorrect. Such distortions can occur for various reasons, including misinformation, suggestion, and the brain's natural tendency to fill in gaps. Essentially, it involves a memory that has been unintentionally or intentionally altered, leading an individual to believe something happened that did not or remember an event in a way that differs from reality.

I begin my text about Jimmy Robert with this anecdote about my youth, with reference to the music industry and Prince, because I see a lot of diverse forms of being, becoming, transitioning, transforming, and mutating—choreographies of change—in Robert's works, which I recognize as artworks but also as living documents. My fall into nostalgia combined with the tricky times we are in, the zeitgeist, form another catalyst for bringing Prince in as a creative mind, artistic aura and reference point. I want to ask how we can look at Robert's moving images, projections, prints, performances, photographs, and installations in relation to the spectacularity of the human body.

Before discussing some of Jimmy Robert's works, let me start with the foundation of his practice. Queer performance offers a space for exploration, self-expression, and subversion of traditional norms, often challenging societal expectations around gender, sexuality, and identity. Through forms such as drag and burlesque, queer performance allows for the celebration and examination of diverse experiences within the LGBTQ+ community. It can be a powerful tool within activism, artistry, and storytelling, creating space for marginalized voices and pushing boundaries in the arts.

Robert's work is subtly critical of racial discrimination; its thoughtful exploration of complex issues has the power to unite many unprivileged subjects. He is not afraid of addressing the impacts of racial and gendered biases, and he always invites viewers to consider their perspectives and assumptions. Using his own body as mental space, subject matter, and object of desire in his performances and installations, he raises conceptual questions about visibility, representation, and power dynamics, particularly for marginalized people and muted communities. His practice provides a lens through which to examine and critique how race, discrimination, and body politics intersect in contemporary culture.

In Yekaterinburg during the preparations for the 6th Ural Biennial, we shared a production process for new works for the first time. For me, being part of the auditions for the performance *Under Amour* (2021) and seeing the series of photographs develop was a learning curve. Robert has such a good nose for smelling the air, alchemy, and chemistry; we were surrounded by young people hungry for any information or input from the internationals and open to any new trick to learn to narrate their own stories.

Now I am looking at that Prince video, "When Doves Cry," again, and reading many sexual references, symbols, mirroring effects, and doubled images, among other flamboyant, arty, ostentatious, and glamorous moments: early queer, camp, and uncanny references in a mainstream video produced for the MTV culture of its time. What Prince does is significant in terms of art's power to play with our imaginations, memories, our channels of remembering and forgetting, as well as our perception of bodies and our self-image.

Controversy is the title of his 1981 album and it was truly controversial.[4] Some critics and fans found the boundary-pushing androgynous image that Prince represented at that point difficult, while the title track addresses several topics, including sex and religion, that have been and continue to be separated in many private spaces. The explicit lyrics and provocative themes in

4 It's an open question for me what pronoun to use for Prince, *he* or *they*? His songs resonate with emotions and experiences that align with a non-binary identity, contributing to the broader conversation about gender expression and identity in today's society.

other songs on the album also contributed. For instance, "Ronnie, Talk to Russia" reflects the political climate of its time, addressing the tensions between the United States and Russia during the Cold War with a plea for peaceful dialogue.

Jimmy Robert's solo exhibition *All dressed up and nowhere to go* took place where I work, as part of our program. In one of the unforgettable moments of the exhibition's promenade, the viewer could not miss a photographic print lit by a strong spot which frequently went dark for a few minutes. In the print, the artist's hands hold open a page for the viewer showing the word "AIDS" written in black on a black-painted background: a work by General Idea. *All dressed up and nowhere to go* sought to trace Robert's previous decade along themes of gender, race, and the politics of representation. For instance, in his 2019 video work *Cruising*, shot in Bucharest, five performers walk from the People's House to the Cathedral of National Salvation, along the thin red line between politics and religion, as a queer act of resistance. Robert is interested in history, not because he is concerned about the past, but because he is interested in a future understanding of silenced, muted, and repressed minorities who share similar stories, songs, and memories of solidarity and survival. As Leo Bersani has put it in reference to Michel Foucault: "power aims to produce subjects defined (and, correlatively, made visible and controlled) by particular desires."[5]

In Robert's video installation *Vanishing Point* (2013), text-based imagination and performativity unfold through architecture and bodily empowerment. Projecting a loop of public performance, a drag queen whips her hair fiercely in Brazilian bate-cabelo style as a voice reads poetry by Ana Cristina César, creating a conceptual link between how we forget and how we remember; it starts with the line: "Lyricism *is the translation of a subjective, sincere personal sentiment*."[6]

In the early stages of establishing our program in Baden-Baden, we found Robert's video *Paramètres* (2011) inspiring—it was also part of *State as≤nd Nature*, our inaugural exhibition, in summer 2021. That was the first time *Paramètres* was exhibited with the presence of the paper sculptures from the video. The phrase "set up the parameters, adjust the structure"—said in his powerful, magical, and clear voice—has become a motto for us in our quest to become more and more resilient.

Several notable works by Jimmy Roberts have been included in politically charged discussions within the contemporary art world. One of his most celebrated exhibitions is *Vis-à-vis*, shown at the Museum of Contemporary Art in Chicago in 2012: a performance and installation

5 Leo Bersani and Adam Phillips, *Intimacies* (University of Chicago Press, 2008).

6 Ana Cristina César, "Primeira Lição" (1979, translation by the poet).

that create a thought-provoking exploration of the relationship between the body, personal history, and cultural identity, using diverse artistic mediums. Additionally, I adore *Draw the Line* (2013), featuring delicate pencil drawings on images from fashion magazines, which has also received significant acclaim for its commentary on representation, race, and gender within mainstream media. With a ribbon, a broken letter typography, or an accent symbol, Robert generates unique gestures that are part of his composition and conceptual thinking but also innovative, critical, and personal forms of expression.

I would like to acknowledge Yusuf Etiman and his Berlin-based open studio space Basso from the mid-2000s, where I met Ian White. Together, Robert and White pushed the boundaries of artistic expression, confronting us with the expectations and conventional norms of the art world. *Joie noire* (2019) is a performance Robert manifested as an homage to Ian White. Its power lies in its relationship with how the oral history of the gender revolution is a living form of shared destiny and faith. Blackouts of memory and sensitive body movements within curated darkness generate spaces for the audience, through imagination, to free themselves from existing norms.

Seeing a work by Jimmy Robert is an opportunity to slow down the mechanisms that imprison us in our current cages; his work is liberating and emancipating, it frees us from boxes, prejudices, and stereotypes. Like

Prince songs, his works bring me resilience, empowerment, and self-confidence. To end this text, I feel like recalling a line from one of Prince's greatest hits: "If the elevator tries to bring you down / go crazy, punch a higher floor." "Let's Go Crazy" (1984), another song written four decades ago and still fresh.

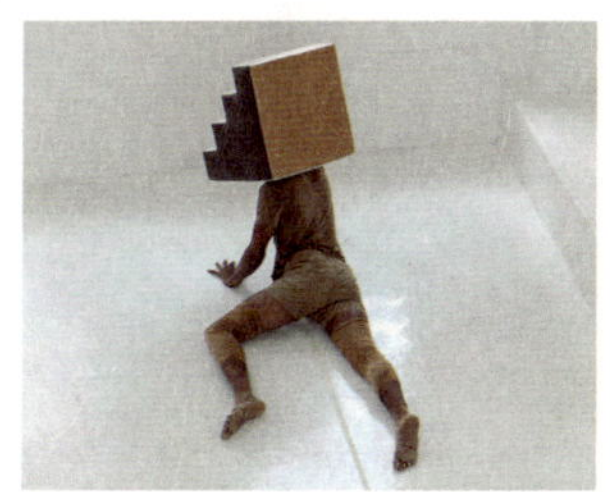

Descendances du nu, 2016

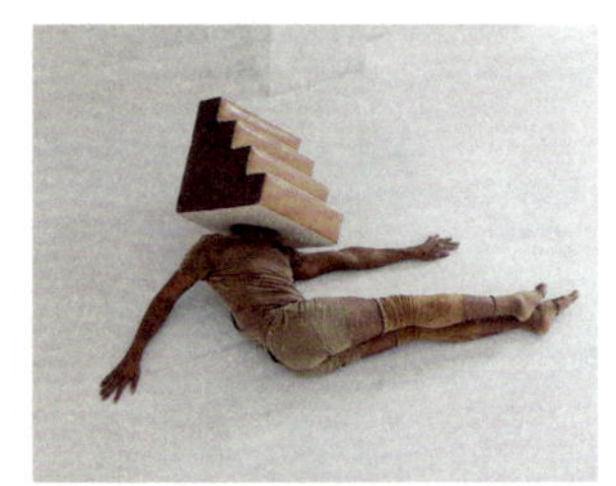

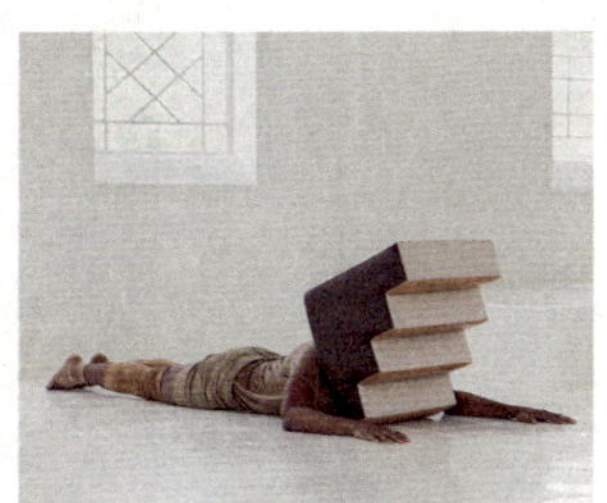

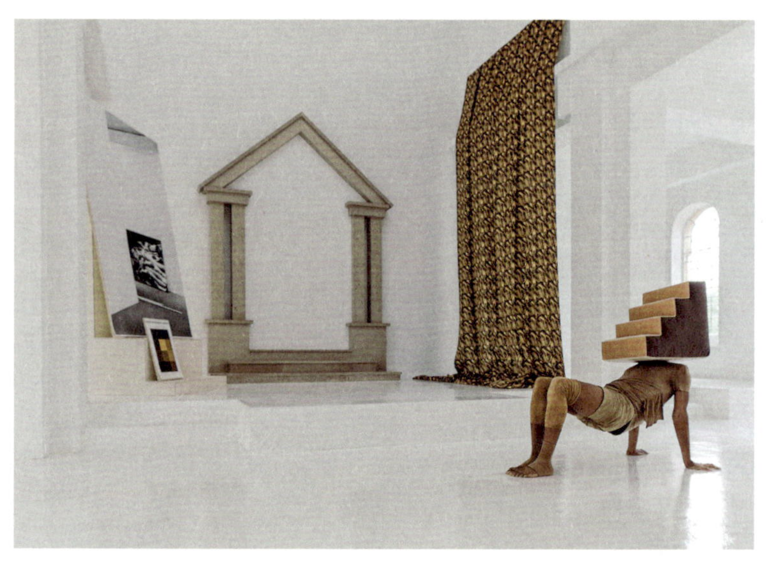

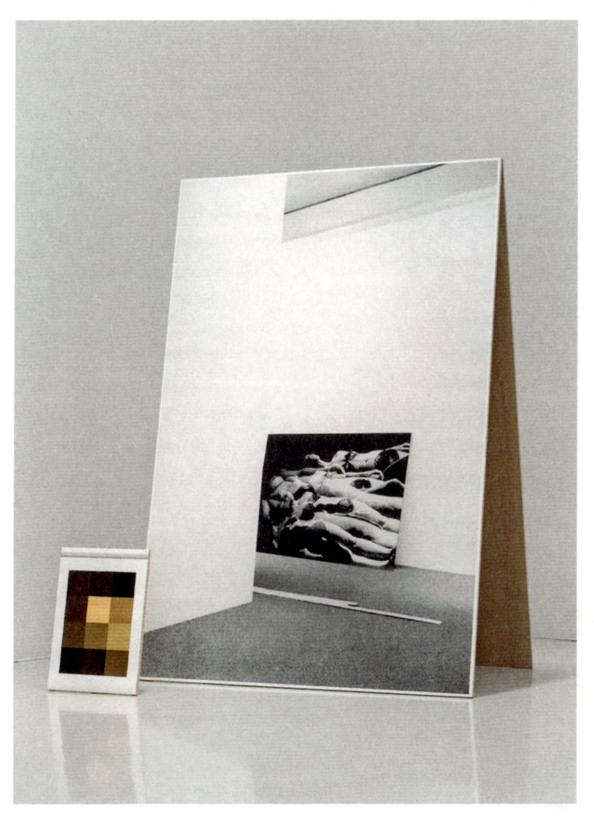

Descendances du nu, 2016

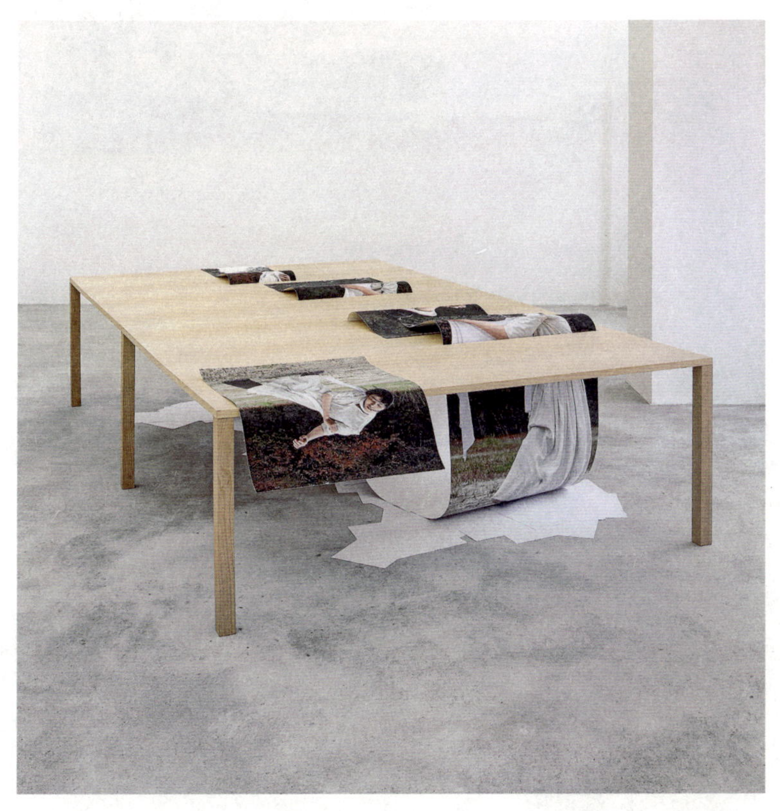

Reprise, 2010

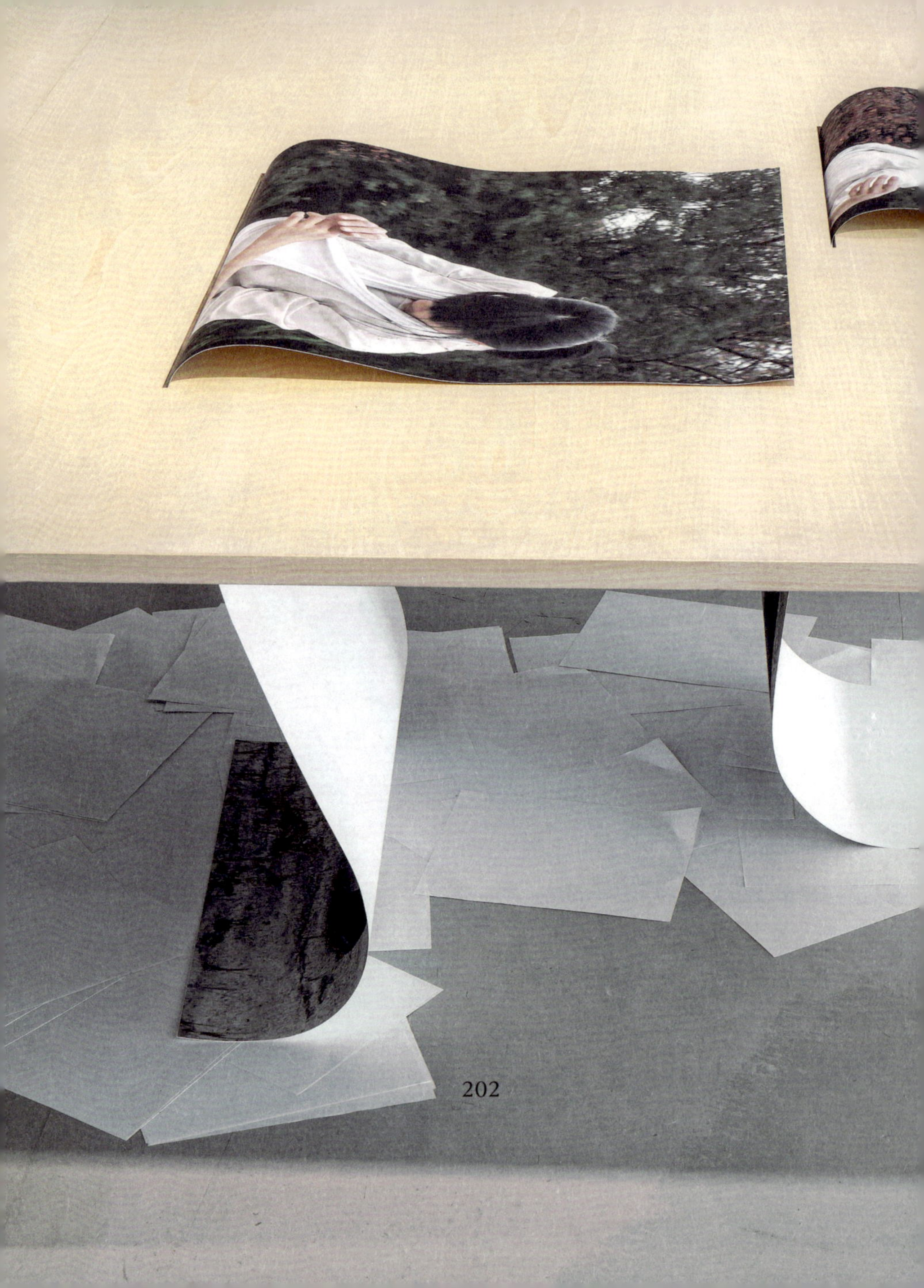

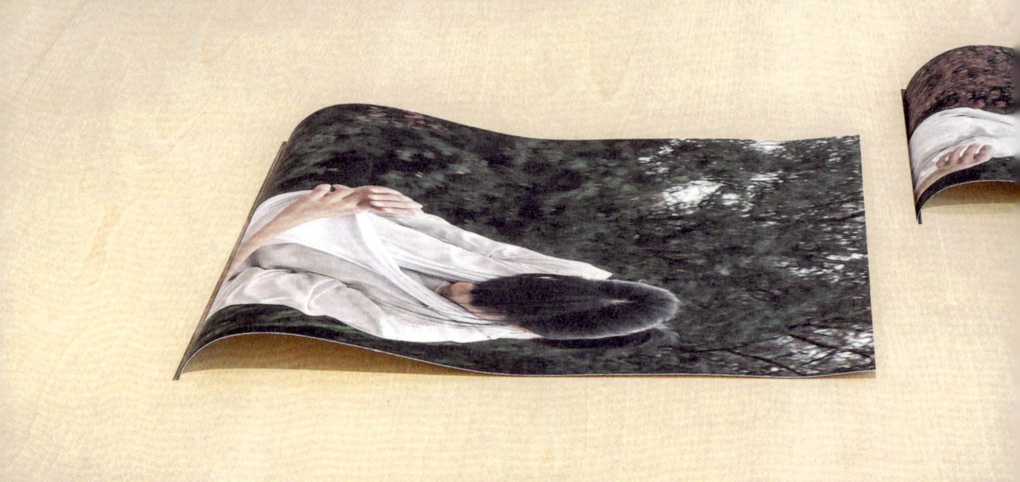

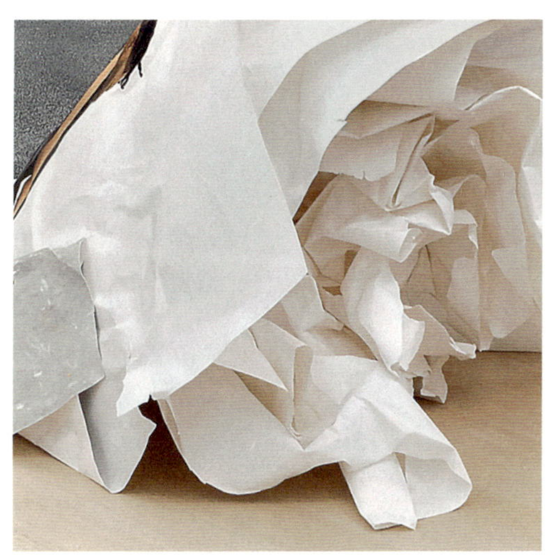

Plié VII, 2021

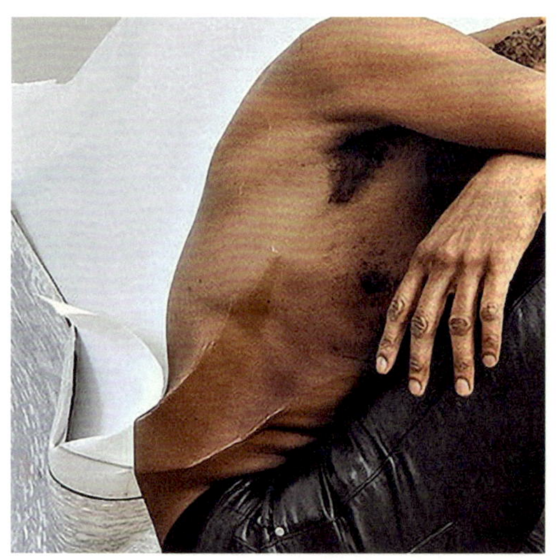

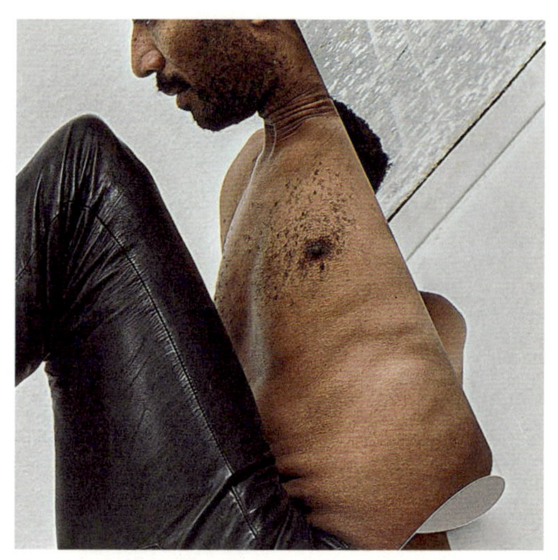

Plié IV, 2021

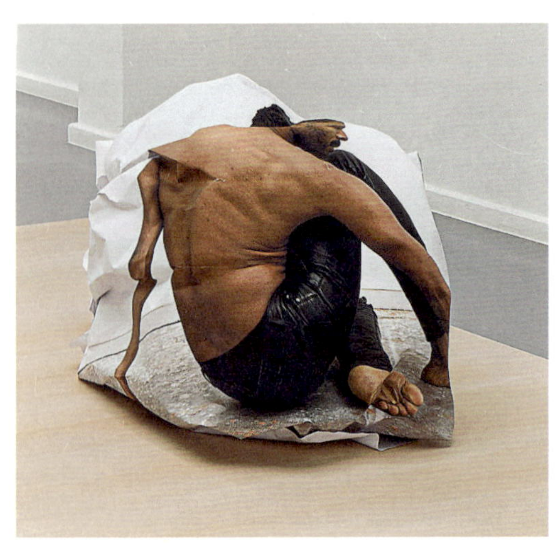

Plié V, 2021

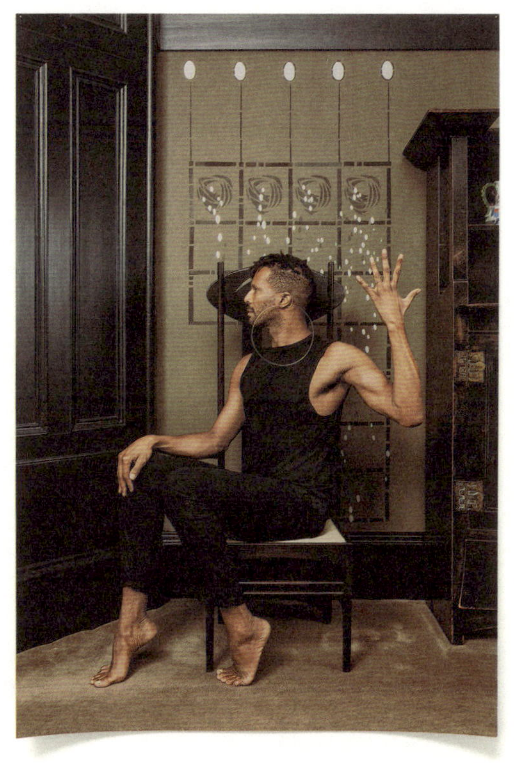

Creole Earring II, 2021

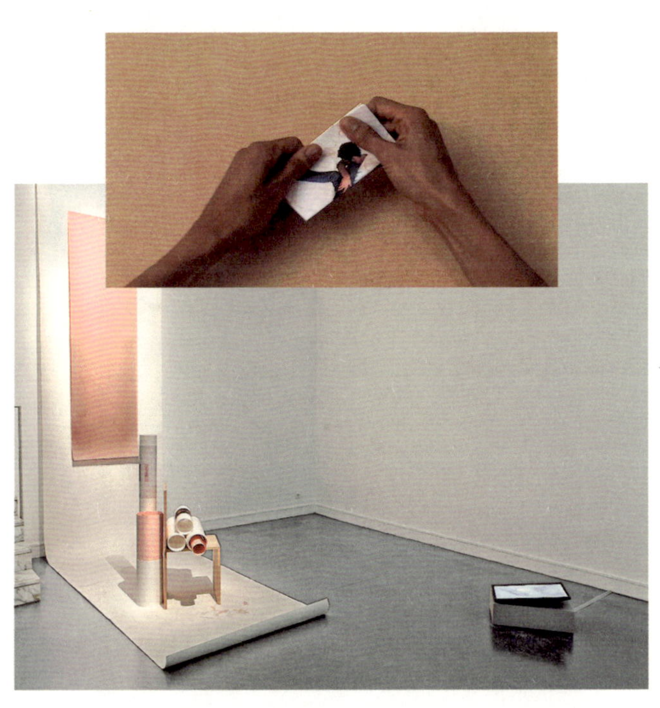

Untitled (Folding II), 2012

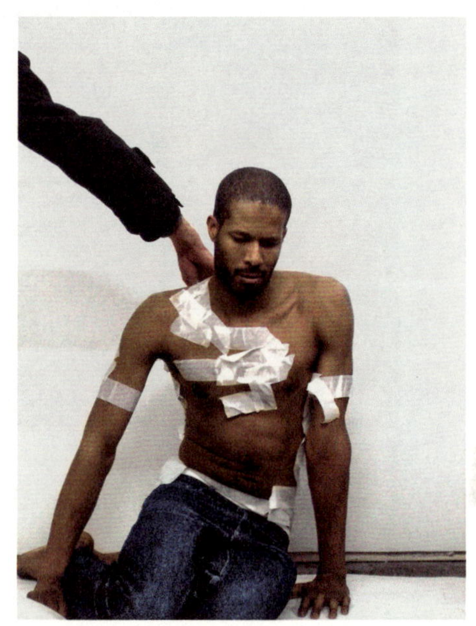

Figure de Style, 2008

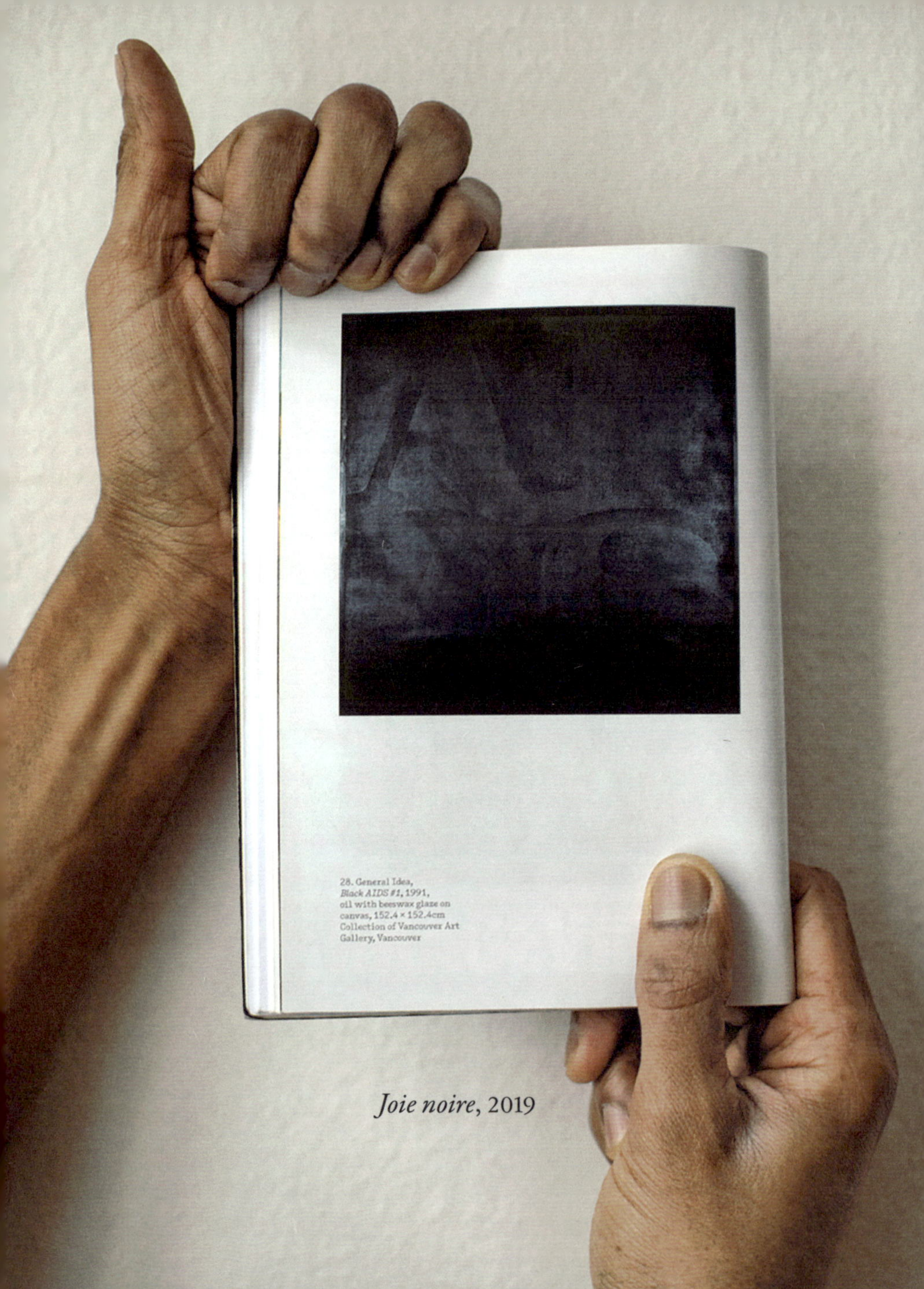

Joie noire, 2019

Three times only.

Jimmy Robert

I am writing from a tiny Parisian hotel and this may have influenced the title. Thinking of one-night stands, and people who refuse to meet more than once even though they had a great time, and for some stupid rule that they haven't taken the time to reflect on. Three is the number of works we made together.

Last weekend I fell into a K-hole thinking of you, maybe because you had shown films at the Lab [the Lab. oratory, Berghain]. Anyway, I thought that would be a great way to start this letter. Ten years have gone since you went. And with those years, the sarcasm, the wit, the dialogue, the acid driblets, the scandalous sex, the experimental drugs ... well, maybe not all of it.

Writing this is harder than I thought, as it forces a reflection that I may have been blissfully resisting. What does it mean to work together and then alone? To go from duo to solo and to establish various forms of collaboration that allow the continuity of a certain dialogue?

A necessary dialogue to keep things in check, avoid complacency...

Let's go chronologically, incrementally:

6 things we couldn't do, but can do now, or when we allowed ourselves to become dancers without being trained. I remember someone distinctly saying to us: "How dare you dance?" Adopting the punk "strategy" of going for what we didn't know with no fear but immense drive, we switched the dynamic of artist/curator to artist/artist. We supported each other in becoming dancers by learning *Trio A* from Yvonne Rainer and Pat Catterson. It felt historical then, it still does. Yvonne came and checked the details of a finger here, the gaze there. We were in awe. It was harder than we had imagined, mostly for being such a so-called democratic dance, but we were fearless. Lean and skinny then, we were "the tall London boys" to her. Turning Yvonne's performance into an object, we danced alongside her on the stage; we were able to look at the choreography in its many facets on a monitor. Like a rough diamond, rock-hard and silent for over an hour. Tight jeans. We danced among many other things: the hanging of a drawing by John Cage, piano playing, moving chairs, a paper dance. Two nights only.

Mariage à la mode et cor anglais. Made for the theater, this piece felt mannered, stylized. Dissecting Roland Barthes and his *Camera Lucida*, the idea of photography and mourning. A portrait of Robert Wilson and Philip Glass by Robert Mapplethorpe. Off we were. Opera blasting, dramatic red curtain, lush robes, leggings, synchronized swimming, and death drops. Death was always around as a theme, as decor, as a drive. It loomed over us. "The AIDS generation," it was said. It did not define us, but it became a form we embraced before it embraced us. Call it empowerment, but with all the elegance of a school play. We went for it shamelessly, rigorously. Rouge noir. "To be alert is to be decorative"—Frank O'Hara.

Some time passed, separate practices emerged. You went on to do three wonderful pieces of your own: *IBIZA, Black Flags*, and *Democracy*. I will always regret not seeing them at the DAAD in Berlin but was very happy to catch *Trauerspiel 1* at HAU. I noticed your wink/homage there, continuing the dialogue in a way only we could see because of working together: recurring forms, colors, and a red-rose bouquet.

Lemon Rose completed the circle somehow, finding us in the place where we first met: the cinema auditorium. Bringing us back to the London days, at LUX when you showed my overly romantic Super-8 films shot in Paris with my family, my home movies. We used the films of Lis Rhodes (*Dresden Dynamo*) and Hollis Frampton (*Lemon*) to establish a double self-portrait, questioning language through movement, text, and overlapping voices, and driving the projectionist of the Jeu de

Paume mad. We commented on experimental cinema while walking, cruising, and interviewing each other in the auditorium. We dissected ourselves in front of an audience in French and English while spraying perfume delicately on each seat. It was the scent of freshly cut grass—bucolic and pedestrian at once, our quality. We broke down our relationship with the screen in order to better define our roles in relation to movement, image, and moving image. We wanted to challenge the expectations linked with an auditorium such as that of the Jeu de Paume. We seemed interchangeable for a moment. Were we?

When you work with someone else you could say you're in a constant state of provocation. You challenge yourself, get to the places where you expect to find the other. Surprise! They sometimes come and join you in sites where you expected resistance. They can also punch you—then you punch them back. Together you move forward, you support and elevate each other. You borrow vocabularies and construct new languages and idiosyncratic gestures: winks/homages to each other.

Every work I make, I hear your voice or at least I think I do. I need to keep the conversation going. Isn't it the only way we do things? Creating imaginary discussions, conflicts, and arguments... After all these years, the sound of you speaking still resonates, not just through my body but many others. Echoes filling the void.

I was not asked to write this text, I put myself in a situation of having to do it. I was missing the dialogue that isn't a dialogue anymore. Bouncing back aimlessly but seriously.

I can hear your laugh or maybe see the beginning of a slight sneer. I wish this was a form of ventriloquism.

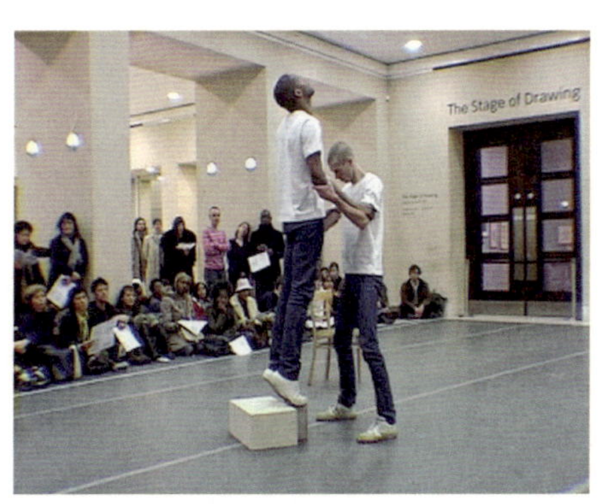

Jimmy Robert/Ian White
6 things we couldn't do, but can do now, 2004

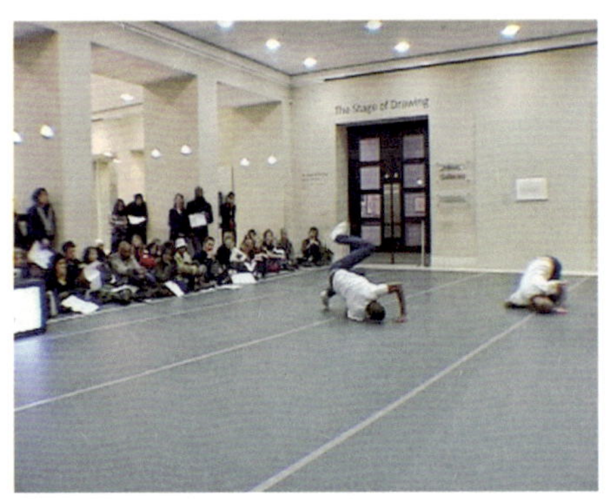
The Stage of Drawing

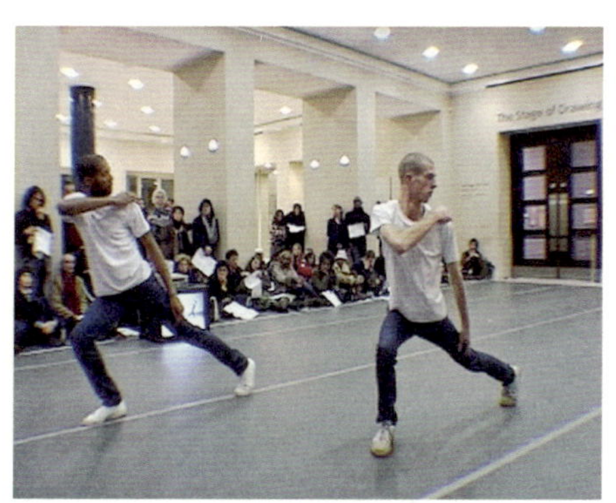

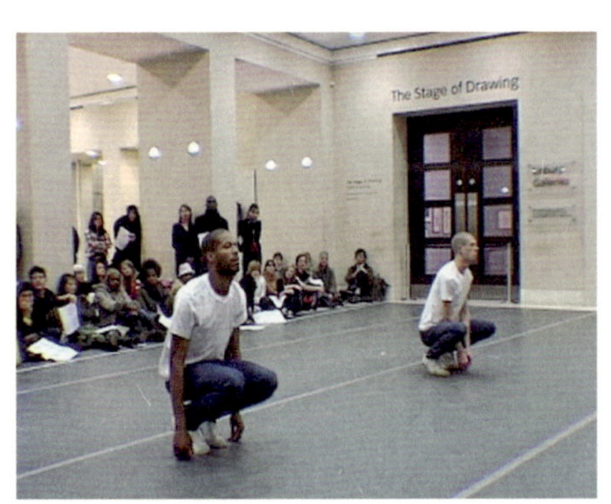
The Stage of Drawing

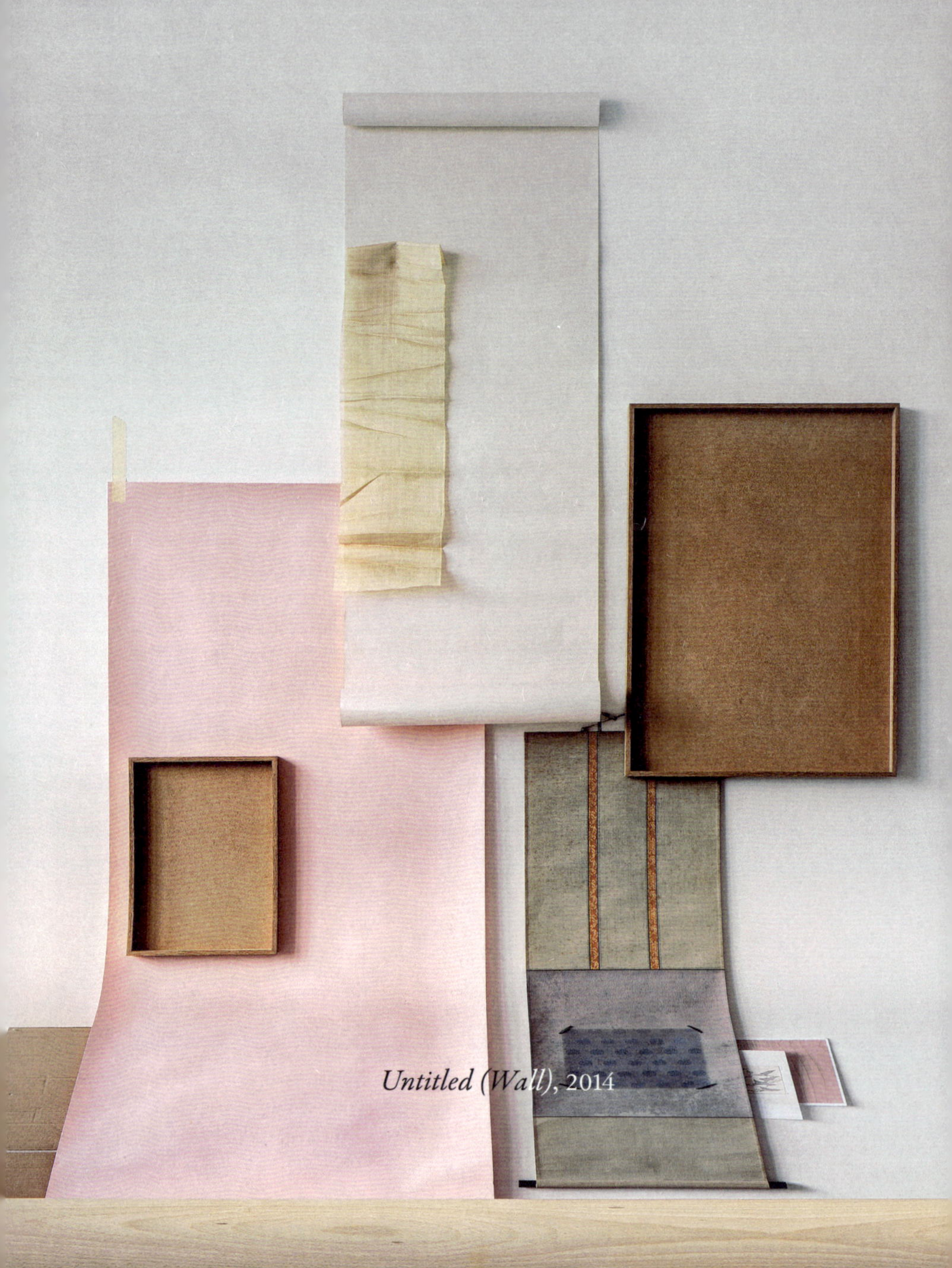

Untitled (Wall), 2014

9
Untitled (Tillmans), 2018
Archival inkjet print, paper
29.7 × 21 cm

10
Untitled (Cork), 2018
Collage on paper
29.7 × 21 cm

11
Untitled (Masking tape), 2018
Tape, paper
29.7 × 21 cm

12
Untitled (Leaf), 2018
Collage, oak frame
32.7 × 24 cm

12
Untitled (copper), 2018
Collage on paper
29.7 × 21 cm

13
Untitled (Boy), 2018
Collage, oak frame
with glass
32 × 23.5 cm

14
Untitled (shadows), 2018
Archival inkjet print,
oak frame
61.5 × 24 cm

25
A clean line that starts from the shoulder, 2015
M-Museum,
Leuven, Belgium
Performance documentation
Photography: Dirk Pauwels

26, 27
Silk, 2015
Print on silk
160 × 120 cm

29
Lili Dujourie
Enjambement, 1976,
Cera-collectie bij
M Leuven © Courtesy
Argos, Centre for Art
& Media, Brussels

30–31
You are only aware of a new neutrality that starts from the hip, 2015
Vinyl text on wall
Variable dimensions

32
Idel Ianchelevici
Dédée, Jeune fille, 1951
Adolescent, 1951
Collection Musée
Ianchelevici La Louvière

33
Aegon, 2015
Archival inkjet print
134 × 100 cm

34
Untitled (Wearing Thin), 2015
Archival inkjet print,
oak frame, tape
138 × 106 cm (print)

35–40
Water binds me to your name (text), 2022
Quotes from Derek Walcott; Ralph Ellison, *The invisible man*; Barooz Boochani; Ocean Vuong; Tatiana Flores, *Relational undercurrents*; Tania Brugera, *Migrant Manifesto, petition to Pope Francis*; Abdellah Taia; Kamau Braithwaite; Jason Mena; Nicolas Laughlin; Mahmoud Darwish, *who am I without exile?*; Abdelfattah Kilito, *Je parle toute les langues mais en Arabe*; Wikipedia
Phenomenon 4, Anafi
Performance documentation
Photography: Alexandra Masmanidi

43
Water binds me to your name, 2022
Vynil text on wall
Variable dimensions

44–45
Technique et Sentiment I, 2021
Archival inkjet print, oak batons
110 × 150 cm

46
All dressed up and nowhere to go IV, 2024
Archival inkjet print
150 × 110 cm

47
Untitled (Sebastien), 2006
Archival inkjet print, beech wood plank
50 × 50 cm (print), 150 × 15 × 1 cm (plank)

48
Plié II, 2020
Archival inkjet print, wooden pedestal, pink ribbon
110 × 150 cm (print), 200 × 200 cm (pedestal)

49
It's not lame… it's Lamé (Toronto), 2016
Archival inkjet prints, beech wood table
75 × 150 × 90 cm (table), 70 × 120 cm (print), 23.5 × 90 cm (rolled text)

50
Plié (rehearsal), 2020
Archival inkjet print
29.7 × 42 cm

59
European Portraits, 2017
PEER, London
Performance documentation
Photography: Ollie Hammick

60–61
Metallica, 2018
Museum Boijmans
Van Beuningen, Rotterdam
Performance documentation
Photography:
Sjoerd Kloosterhuis

62
The Mile-Long Paper Walk (1965/2014), 2014
MoMA, New York
Performance documentation
Photography: Julieta Cervantes

63
Abolibibelo, 2015
Migros Museum für
Gegenwartskunst, Zürich
Performance documentation
Photography: Nicolas Duc

64–67
Imitation of Lives, 2017
The Glass House, Performa 17,
New Canaan
Performance documentation
Photography: Mike Biondo

68–70
Old masters, 2019
Evening of Performances,
DRAF × Ministry of Sound,
London
Performance documentation
Photography: Mike Massaro

73
Plié I, 2020
Archival inkjet print,
wooden pedestal
110 × 150 cm (print),
200 × 200 cm (pedestal)

76
Plié IV, 2020
Archival inkjet print,
wooden pedestal
110 × 150 cm (print),
200 × 200 cm (pedestal)

77
Plié III, 2020
Archival inkjet print,
wooden pedestal
110 × 150 cm (print),
200 × 200 cm (pedestal)

78
Paramètres, 2012
HD video, sound
5:20 minutes

99
Untitled (Desk), 2013
Archival inkjet print, oak frame
67 × 50 cm

100–101
Untitled (Skin/Visage), 2013
Two archival ink-jet prints,
oak frame
117.5 × 91 cm (print),
32 × 23 cm (print),
36 × 27 cm (frame)

102
Frammenti VII, 2022
Oak frame with no glass,
archival inkjet print
144 × 94 × 4.3 cm

103
Untitled (Patterns), 2018
archival Inkjet print,
altered oak frame
41 × 22.2 × 31 cm

104–105
Untitled (Belladonna),
2007/2021
Archival inkjet print,
charcoal
65 × 49.5 cm (print)

106–107
Untitled (Ompdrailles), 2013
Archival inkjet print,
turned oak
144 × 97 × 10 cm

108–109
Technique et Sentiment II, 2021
Archival inkjet print,
oak batons
110 × 150 cm

113
Cadavre exquis, 2010
Archival inkjet print
50 × 50 cm

114
Technique et Sentiment V, 2021
Archival inkjet print,
oak batons
150 × 110 cm

131
Technique et Sentiment IV, 2021
Archival inkjet print,
oak batons
150 × 110 cm

132–33
It's not lame... it's Lamé, 2017
Archival inkjet prints
29.7 × 21 cm (each print)

134
It's not lame...it's Lamé (Paris), 2023
Print on fabric
400 × 300 cm

135
Frammenti I, 2022
Archival inkjet print,
oak frame with glass
34 × 25 × 4 cm

136
Frammenti VIII, 2022
Oak frame with no glass,
archival inkjet print
74.7 × 59.5 × 4 cm

137
Untitled (Fragments), 2015
Archival inkjet print, oak frame
101.5 × 73 cm

139
Untitled (skirt study amended), 2011
Various paper on cardboard
116 × 75 cm

141
Under Amour, 2021
Archival inkjet print
110 × 150 cm

143–146
A Davidoff Cigar at Casa de Campo, 2021
Super8 film transferred
to video, color, silent
3:11 minutes

149
Vanishing Point, 2013
2 birch wood structures, paper; 2 Super 8 films transferred to HD video, color and b/w 9 minutes

150, 151
All dressed up and nowhere to go, 2023
Site-specific installation
Collaboration with Diogo Passarinho
Studio Kunsthalle Baden-Baden, Baden-Baden

152
Homage to the young boy, 2007
Ink on paper
29.7 × 21 cm

153–56
Joie noire, 2019
KW Institute for Contemporary Art, Berlin
Performance documentation
Photography: Frank Sperling

163–166
L'éducation sentimentale, 2005
Super 8 film transferred to 35mm film, black and white, colour, silent
5:36 minutes

167
Brown Leatherette, 2002
16mm film, color, silent
5:55 minutes

169–172
French film, 2000
Super 8 film transferred to video, black and white, sound
10:12 minutes

173–176
Cruising, 2019
HD video, colour, sound
11:38 minutes

181
Floorwork, 2020
Silkscreened text on
wood-veneered board
84 × 59 cm

195–199
Descendances du nu, 2016
Centre d'art
contemporain, Delme
Performance documentation
Photography:
O.H. Dancy

201–202
Reprise, 2010
Archival inkjet prints,
paper, fiberboard table
with beech veneer
300 × 180 x 70 cm

203–204
Plié VII, 2021
Archival inkjet print,
wooden pedestal
110 × 150 cm (print),
200 × 200 cm (pedestal)

205
Plié IV, 2020
Archival inkjet print,
wooden pedestal
110 × 150 cm (print),
200 × 200 cm (pedestal)

206
Plié V, 2020
Archival inkjet print,
wooden pedestal
110 × 150 cm (print),
200 × 200 cm (pedestal)

207
Creole Earring II, 2021
Archival inkjet print
110 × 150 cm

208
Untitled (Folding II), 2012
HD video, sound
5:20 minutes

209
Figure de Style, 2008
Cubitt, London
Performance documentation

210
Joie noire, 2019
Archival inkjet print
150 × 110 cm

217–220
Jimmy Robert / Ian White
6 things we couldn't do,
but can do now, 2004
Tate Britain, London
Performance documentation
Photography: Sheila Burnett

222
Untitled (Wall), 2014
Archival inkjet print,
masking tape, beech rod
240 × 52 cm (print),
140 × 10 cm (rod)

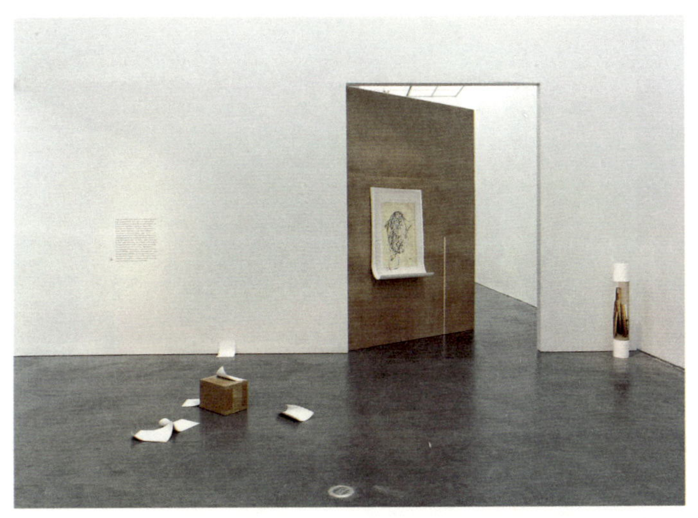

Vis-à-vis, 2012
MCA Chicago, Chicago

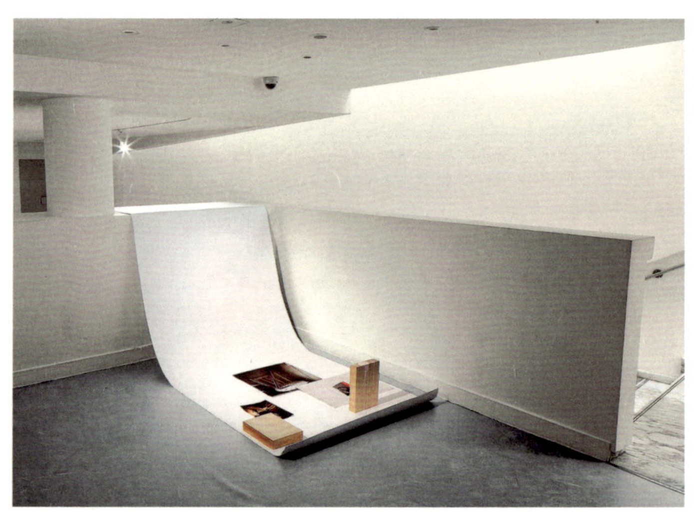

Langue Matérielle, 2012
Jeu de Paume, Paris

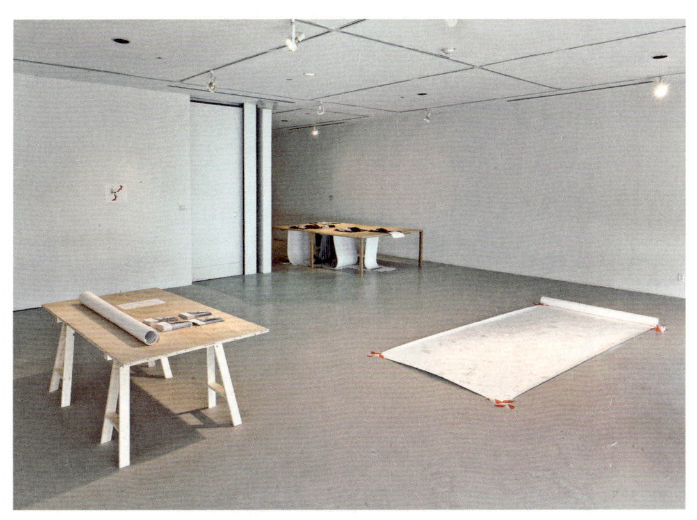

Draw the Line, 2013
The Power Plant, Toronto

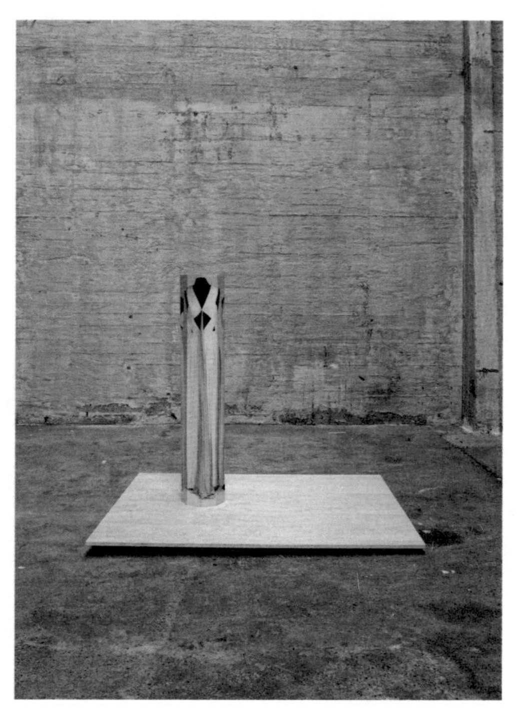

Made to Measure, 2013
1857, Oslo

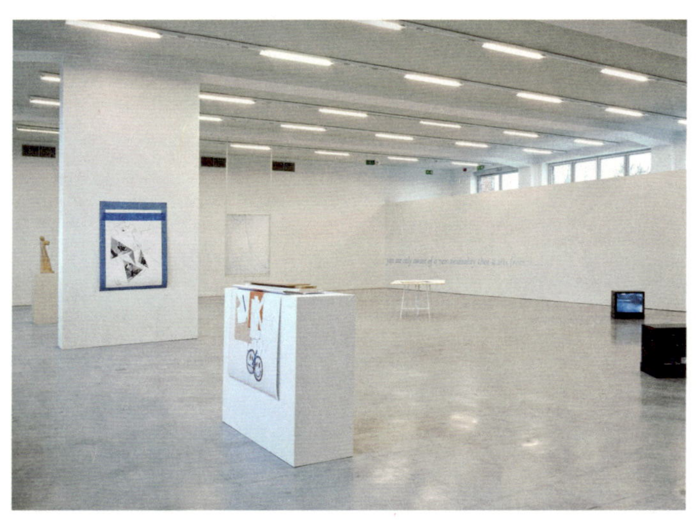

A clean line that starts from the shoulder, 2016
M-Museum, Leuven

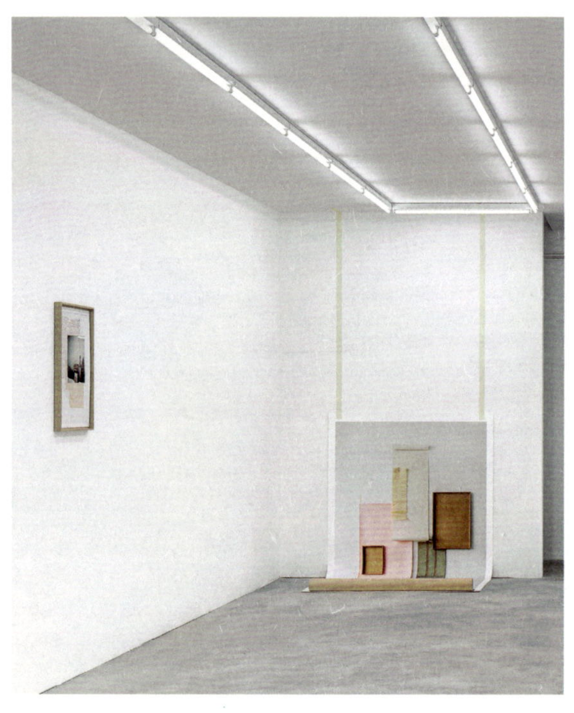

It's not lame, it's Lamé, 2016
Tanya Leighton Gallery, Berlin

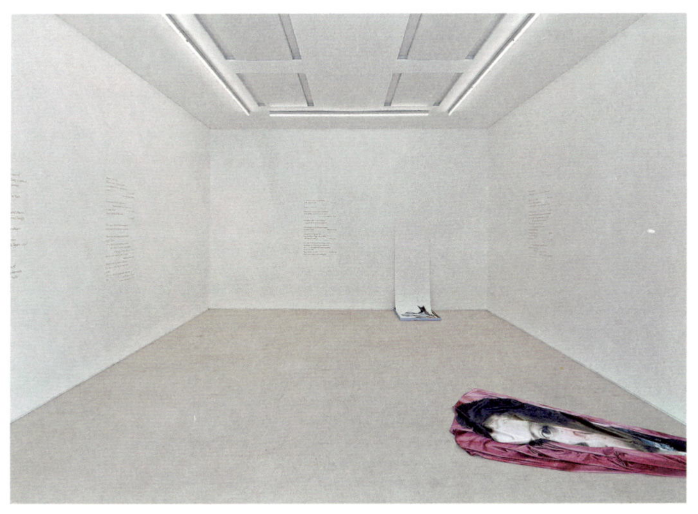

European Portraits, 2017
PEER, London

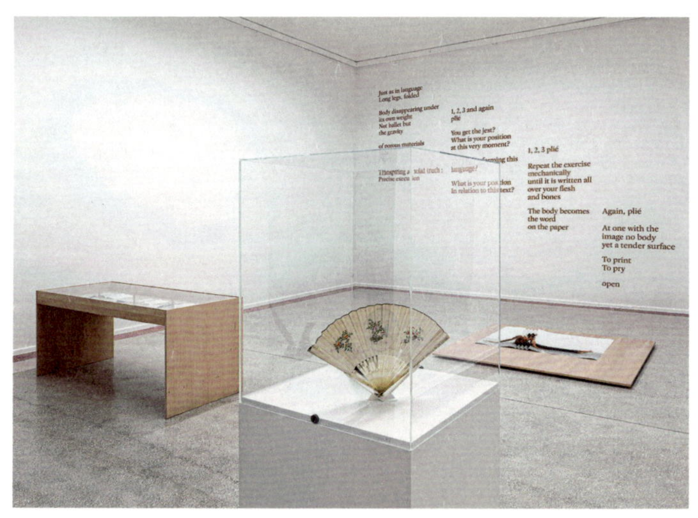

Plié, 2020
Leopold-Hoesch-Museum & Papiermuseum, Düren

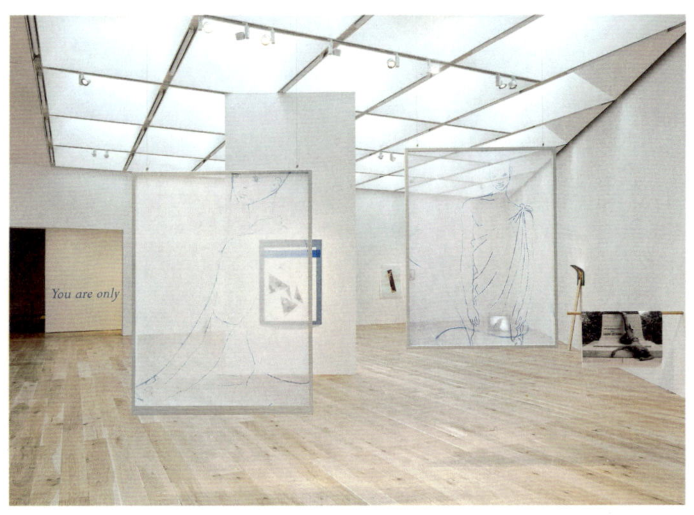

Akimbo, 2021
Nottingham Contemporary

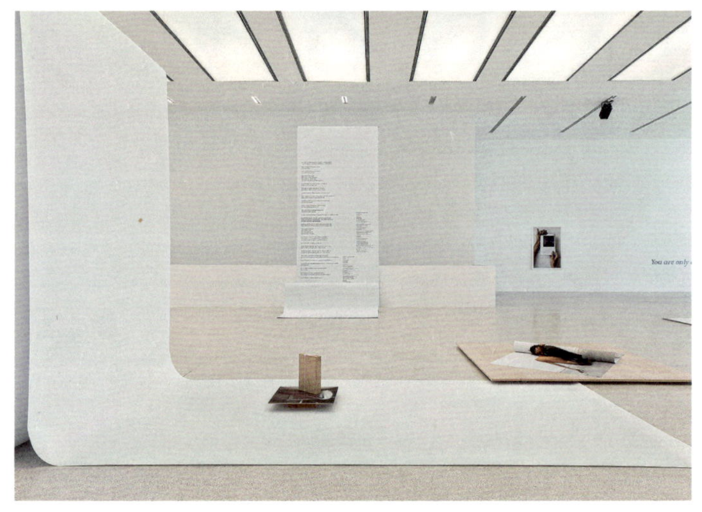

Mirror Language, 2021
Museion, Bolzano

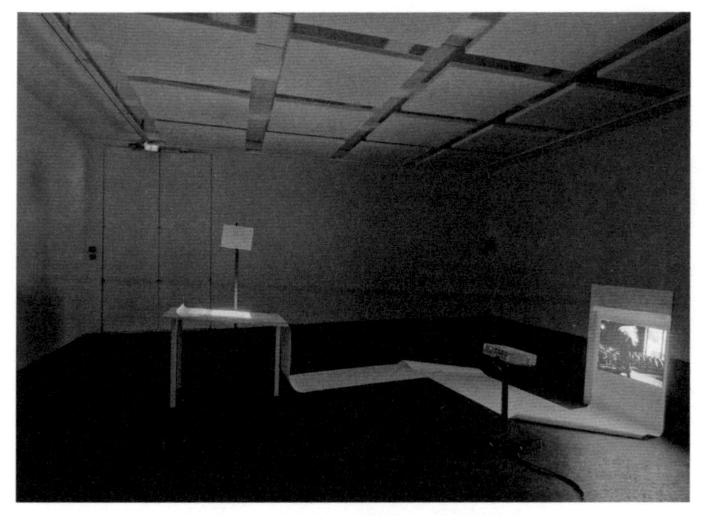

Appui, tendu, renversé, 2022
CRAC Occitanie in Sète

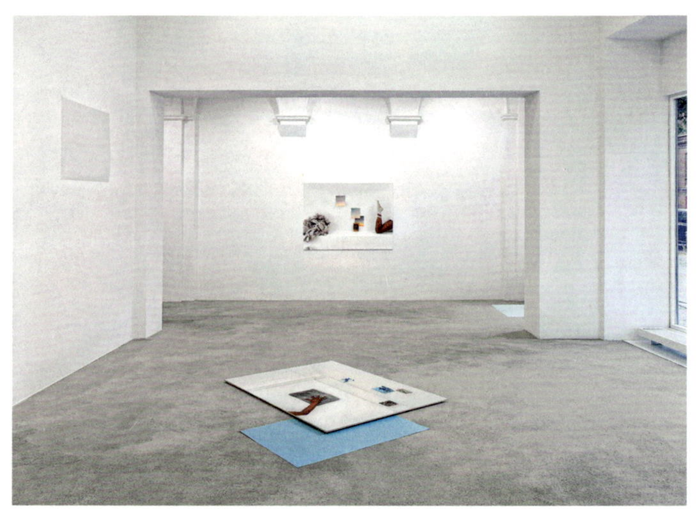

Technique et Sentiment, 2021
Tanya Leighton Gallery, Berlin

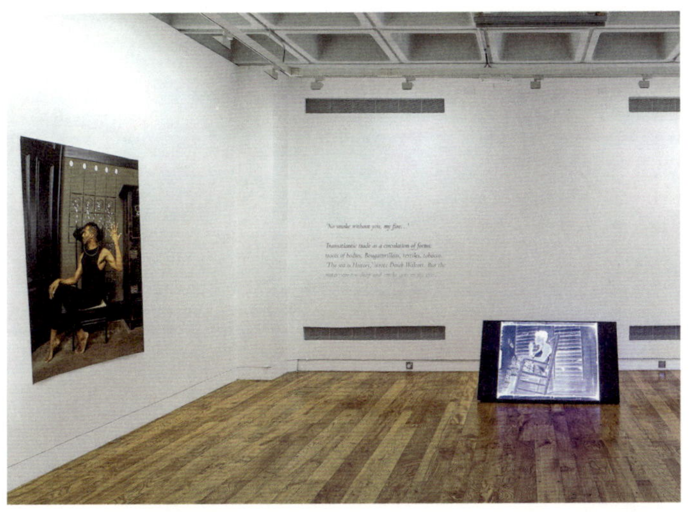

Tobacco Flower, 2021
Hunterian Art Gallery, Glasgow

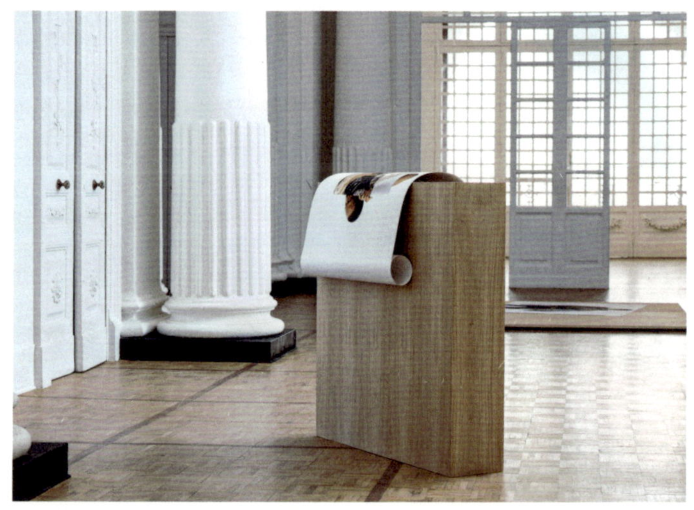

Frammenti, 2022
Thomas Dane Gallery, Naples

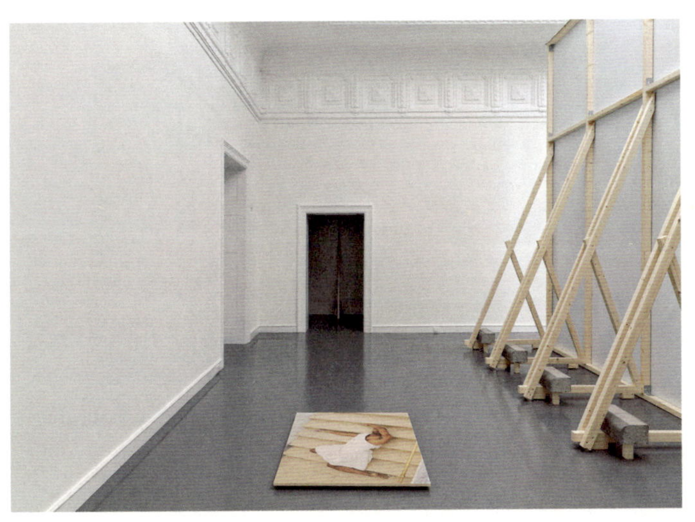

All dressed up and nowhere to go, 2023
Kunsthalle Baden-Baden, Baden-Baden

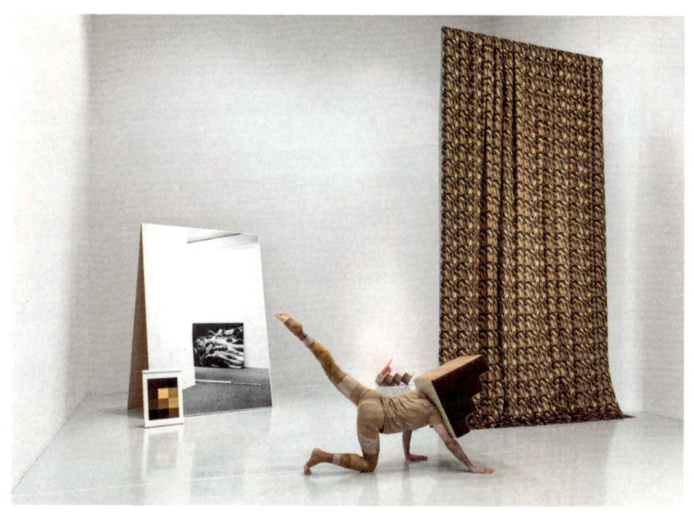

Asymmetrical Grammar, 2023
Moderna Museet, Malmö

Jimmy Robert / Ian White
6 things we couldn't do, but can do now, 2004
Tate Modern, London
Curated by: Catherine Wood

The artists cinema, 2006
Frieze Projects at Frieze Art Fair, London
Curated by: Ian White

Figure de Style, 2008
Cubitt, London
Curated by: Bart Van der Heide

Vis-à-vis, 2012
MCA Chicago, Chicago
Curated by: Naomi Beckwith

Langue Materiélle, 2012
Jeu de Paume, Paris
Curated by: Filipa Oliveira

Draw the Line, 2013
The Power Plant, Toronto
Curated by: Julia Paoli

Made to Measure, 2013
1857, Oslo
Curated by: Stian Eide Kluge and Steffen Håndlykken

The Mile-Long Paper Walk (1965/2014), 2014
James Lee Byars: 1/2 an Autobiography, MoMA PS1, New York
Curated by: Peter Eleey

8th Berlin Biennial, 2014
KW Institute for Contemporay Art, Berlin
Curated by: Juan Gaitan

Abolibibelo, 2015
Migros Museum für Gegenwartskunst, Zurich
Curated by: Raphael Gygax

A clean line that starts from the shoulder, 2015
M-Museum, Leuven
Curated by: Valery Verhack

Descendance du nu, 2016
CAC Synagogue de Delme, Delme
Curated by: Marie Cozette

Imitation of Lives, 2017
Realised for Performa 17
The Glass House, New Canaan
Curated by: Cole Akers and Charles Aubin

European Portraits, 2017
PEER, London
Curated by: Ingrid Svenson

Metallica, 2018
Performed at Boijmans Museum as part of *Prosecute My Posture*
Garage Rotterdam, Rotterdam
Curated by: Sjoerd Kloosterhuis

Joie noire, 2019
Pause, KW Institute for Contemporary Art, Berlin
Curated by: Mason Leaver-Yap

Old Masters, 2019
Evening of Performances by DRAF, Ministry of Sound, London
Curated by: Louise O' Kelly

Cruising, 2019
Displacement and togetherness as part of *Europalia*
Strombeek Museum, Strombeek
Curated by: Salonul de proiecte

Plié, 2020
Leopold-Hoesch-Museum & Papiermuseum, Düren
Curated by: Markus Mascher

Akimbo, 2021
Nottingham Contemporary
Curated by: Nicole Yip

Mirror Language, 2021
Museion, Bolzano
Curated by: Bart Van der Heide and Frida Carazzato

Appui, tendu, renversé, 2021
CRAC Occitanie, Sète
Curated by: Marie Cozette

Tobacco Flower, 2021
Hunterian Art Gallery, Glasgow
Curated by: Dominic Paterson

Under Amour, 2021
Thinking Hands Touching Each Other, Urali Biennal, Ekaterinburg
Curated by: Misal Adnan Yıldız, Çağla Ilk, Assaf Kimmel

Water binds me to your name, 2022
Phenomenon 4, Anafi
Directed by: Iordanis Kerenidis and Piergiorgio Pepe

All dressed up and nowhere to go, 2022
Kunsthalle Baden-Baden, Baden-Baden
Curated by: Christina Lehnert

When I State that I Am an Anarchist, 2022
PLATO Ostrava, Ostrava
Curated by: Pierre Bal Blanc

Pausing, 2023
as part of Exposeé at Palais de Tokyo
Centre National de la Danse, Paris
Curated by: François Piron

Asymmetrical Grammar, 2023
Moderna Museet, Malmö
Curated by: Andreas Nilsson

Jimmy Robert
The Man Who Envied Women

Texts: Kirsty Bell, Çağla Ilk, Bart van der Heide, Élisabeth Lebovici, Karolin Meunier, Magnus Elias Rosengarten, Misal Adnan Yıldız

Editor: Nadja Abt

Image editor: Roberta Cotterli

Copy editor: Jenifer Evans

Graphic design: Stoodio Santiago da Silva, Ana Cecilia Breña

Lithography: Jan Scheffler, Print Professional

Published by
Bierke Verlag, Berlin
bierke.de

ISBN 978-3-948546-15-1
Printed in Europe by Gutenberg Beuys Feindruckerei

This publication was made possible through the generous support of Senatsverwaltung für Kultur und Gesellschaftlichen Zusammenhalt Berlin, Fluxus Art Projects, and Staatliche Kunsthalle Baden-Baden.

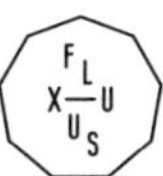

STAATLICHE KUNSTHALLE
BADEN—BADEN

Additional support was given by Tanya Leighton, Thomas Dane, Stigter van Doesburg, Daniel Lieberberg, Iordanis Kereddenis/Piergiorgio Pepe, and Matthias Hartmann.

Jimmy Robert would like to thank:
Nadja Abt; Bakri Bakhit; Kirsty Bell; Ana Cecilia Breña; Faye Campbell; Frida Carazzato; Roberta Cotterli; Marie Cozette; Thomas Dane; Tom Dingle; Jenifer Evans; Fluxus Art Projects; Melanie Garcia; gOlab Berlin, Christine Fenzl and Susanna Kirschnick; Matthias Hartmann; Bart van der Heide; Çağla Ilk; Misal Adnan Yıldız; Iordanis Kerenidis and Piergiorgio Pepe; Élisabeth Lebovici; Tanya Leighton; Daniel Lieberberg; Matthias Mau; Karolin Meunier; Motor Dance Journal, Isabelle Bucklow and Hannah Woods; Hélène Nguyen-Ban; Magnus Elias Rosengarten; Yvonne Rainer; Santiago da Silva; Staatliche Kunsthalle Baden-Baden; Diana Stigter; Paula Vogels; Ian White; Nicole Yip; Zheng Zhang

Distribution:

Public Knowledge Books, UK/EU
bryony@publicknowledgebooks.com

NBN, USA/CA
nbnbooks.com
customercare@nbnbooks.com

Les presses du réel,
FR/B/L/CH
lespressesdureel.com
info@lespressesdureel.com

GVA Göttingen, GER
gva-verlage.de
rabe@gva-verlage.de

Nationalbibliothek lists this publication in the Deutsche Nationalbibliografie. Detailed bibliographic data is available online at http://dnb.de.

Text Credits:

The title "The Man Who Envied Women" is borrowed from the 1985 film of the same name, as an homage to Yvonne Rainer's work, with kind permission from the artist: *"The Man Who Envied Women sees Rainer, in her own words, "throw down the gauntlet to psychoanalytic feminist film theory," interrogating and responding to contemporary debates over notions such as the male gaze with a drolly provocative hybrid essay film. Rainer's account of the break-up of a marriage between a womanizing blowhard Manhattan professor (played alternately by William Raymond and Larry Loonin) and his artist wife, who exists only as voice-over (choreographer Trisha Brown), soon galaxy brains outwards to address concerns as divergent as the housing crisis facing New York artists and political struggles in Latin America."* (source: https://zeitgeist-films.com/film/manwhoenviedwomen)

Bart van der Heide, "Mirror Language," first published in the context of the exhibition "Jimmy Robert: Mirror Language," Museion Bolzano, 29 May–22 August 2021; with kind permission of the author.

Élisabeth Lebovici, "En descendant," first published in the context of the exhibition "Descendances du nu," Centre d'art contemporain–la synagogue de Delme, Metz, 18 June–25 September 2016; with kind permission of the author.

Karolin Meunier, "Affectional Leaps," a shorter version of this text was published online at www.textezurkunst.de, 22 January 2019; with kind permission of the author.

Jimmy Robert, "Three Times Only," text commissioned by motor dance journal (eds. Isabelle Bucklow and Hannah Woods) for "Duets and Dialogues" (Issue 2, November 2023); with kind permission of motor dance journal.